TREASON
IN AMERICA

OTHER BOOKS BY JULES ARCHER

African Firebrand:
    Kenyatta of Kenya

Angry Abolitionist:
    William Lloyd Garrison

Battlefield President:
    Dwight D. Eisenhower

Colossus of Europe:
    Metternich

Congo

The Dictators

The Executive "Success"

The Extremists:
    Gadflies of American Society

Fighting Journalist:
    Horace Greeley

Front-Line General:
    Douglas MacArthur

Hawks, Doves, and the Eagle

Indian Foe, Indian Friend

Laws That Changed America

Man of Steel:
    Joseph Stalin

Philippines' Fight for Freedom

Red Rebel:
    Tito of Yugoslavia

Science Explorer:
    Roy Chapman Andrews

Thorn in Our Flesh:
    Castro's Cuba

Twentieth-Century Caesar:
    Benito Mussolini

The Unpopular Ones

World Citizen:
    Woodrow Wilson

TREASON IN AMERICA

DISLOYALTY VERSUS DISSENT

by Jules Archer

HAWTHORN BOOKS, INC.   PUBLISHERS   NEW YORK

2   3   4   5   6   7   8   9   10

To Kerry Russell Archer
at Harvard

Contents

TREASON
IN AMERICA

1   WHAT IS TREASON?

"Treason," according to the *Encyclopedia Americana,* is "the breach of the allegiance which a person owes to the state under whose protection he lives, and the most serious crime known to the law." But exactly what does it mean to be guilty of a "breach of the allegiance" owed to your country? Since treason is punishable by the death penalty, the prosecution is required to prove that anyone indicted as a traitor is indeed an enemy of his country, both by intention and deed, not simply an idealistic patriot who wants to oust the incumbent administration because he sincerely believes it is misruling the country he loves.

Should our view of treason, and the punishment we prescribe, distinguish between those who are disloyal out of high motives and those who are traitors for greed or ambition?

Should we condemn as base not only Aaron Burr and Benedict Arnold, who were traitors for personal gain, but also those Americans who collaborate with a foreign power because they sincerely believe in the superiority of the principles espoused by that alien nation?

Should we punish equally the government employee who sells military secrets to foreign spies for large sums of money and the physicist who reveals atomic secrets to scientists outside the country because he believes in international scientific cooperation as the only path to world peace and progress?

Every major power in the world operates a secret intelligence service to pry out the secrets of unfriendly nations. Ours is the C.I.A. No country, including our own, lacks some citizens who are willing, for a price or out of hostility toward their government, to turn over its secrets or to engage in subversive activities under foreign direction.

In determining whether an American citizen has committed treason, we require valid evidence, as well as two witnesses or a confession in open court; knowledge of the reasons for such treason; and also knowledge of how much harm it has actually done the country.

It is not always as simple as it seems to decide what is, or is not, treason. Let's become jurors considering some typical cases drawn from real life.

Imagine that the citizen who comes before us admits that during the recent war he had blown up one of the nation's munition factories. An obvious act of treason!

But what if this is now postwar France, and the defendant has been a guerrilla of the French underground, sabotaging the collaborationist Vichy Government? True, he was a traitor to Vichy France. But in our eyes he was a patriotic Frenchman fighting French traitors who had sold out his country to the German enemy. Our whole perspective about the case is now dramatically reversed. Not guilty!

The next case on our docket deals with a soldier in the field who has refused to obey government orders and has even killed the officer who tried to compel him to obey. Treason!

But what if this is Germany during World War II? The Nazi Government has ordered the mass extermination of all Jews and

Slavs, including women and children. The defendant is a German soldier who puts loyalty to his God and his conscience above loyalty to the state. Is he a traitor to his country? Or is he a patriot who refuses to besmirch German honor by obeying an order to commit crimes against humanity?

The judges at the Nuremberg Trials declared that it is not treason to defy a government order to commit atrocities, but it is in fact treason to humanity to carry out such orders.

Let's consider a few other paradoxes that indicate the importance of motivation in deciding what we can justly label as treason.

In the dark a man suddenly springs out of some bushes and without warning kills three men strolling along a road. Murder! But wait—he wears an American officer's uniform. He has just slain three enemy soldiers in a country we are fighting. A hero!

But the light is better now, and we discover our mistake. The officer belongs to the enemy; the three soldiers he has ambushed are ours. Treachery!

Then it turns out, after all, that he *is* one of our officers. He has thwarted the attempt of three American deserters to escape to the enemy. A patriot!

But we next learn that he attacked the soldiers because they had discovered his plan to lead a military putsch to take over the U.S. Army and were about to expose him. Traitor!

Motivation, obviously, has a great deal to do with whether someone can be considered a traitor or patriot. What is considered treason in one light can be recognized as patriotism in another. Much depends on *who* is doing the judging—also where; also when. The reasons why a man turns against his government may range all the way from the sordid motive of selling out his country for a bribe to opposing the administration for what he believes to be betrayal of his country's traditions and ideals.

The problem of defining treason is so complicated that many

Americans confuse it with political opposition to the Government, especially when dissent takes the form of breaking the law as a symbolic protest.

In a country which guarantees freedom of speech and dissent to all citizens, the limits to which dissent may be carried before an American is subject to arrest are problematical. But so is the question of treason when applied to a manufacturer who seeks excess profits by supplying the Army with inferior weapons that malfunction in battle.

Treason, obviously, would seem far too serious a charge to be leveled at any American except for the gravest of reasons. Yet it has often been hurled, as we shall see, for the political purpose of character assassination.

Abraham Lincoln had some thoughts on what is *not* treason in his first inaugural address. "This country with its institutions belongs to the people who inhabit it," he told the American people. "Whenever they shall grow weary of the existing Government, they can exercise their constitutional right of amending it or their revolutionary right to dismember or overthrow it."

We are, after all, a nation founded in revolution, which is justified in the Declaration of Independence. Many other governments in the world also hold power today because of revolutions against previous regimes. A few of these are the Soviet Union, Spain, Yugoslavia, Greece, Cuba, Mexico, Indonesia, Red China, France, Germany, Italy, Ireland, South Vietnam, North Vietnam, the Philippines, Egypt, Iraq, Cambodia, the Congo, and almost all of Central and South America.

Traitors, ironically, are considered traitors only so long as their treason is unsuccessful. "Treason doth never prosper," noted English writer Sir John Harington in 1613. "What's the reason? For if it prosper, none dare call it Treason!"

Those British subjects who wrote the Declaration of Independence were only traitors until their treason succeeded. Then they became the new authority in America, clothed in every bit as much respectability as the British governors whom they overthrew. And we now respect them as our great patriots.

Many Americans today feel, however, that revolution is no longer necessary or justified since we now have a two-party political system, in which the party out of power becomes the legitimate focus of grievances against the Government. Certainly our history proves that the minority party has functioned as a bitter critic and foe of the administration in power.

But sometimes *both* major parties support a controversial venture, such as the Vietnam war. At such times the frustration of large numbers of Americans becomes so great as to explode in violent opposition to the government, as occurred during the turbulent election campaign year of 1968.

The citizen driven to defiance of the government out of dedication to principle does not regard himself as disloyal but as a true patriot. When Brutus joined the plot to assassinate Caesar, he insisted, "Not that I loved Caesar less, but that I loved Rome more."

Often when a revolutionist wins power, he sets up revolutionary courts to try those government officials he has overthrown as "traitors to the country." (Fidel Castro, Francisco Franco, Marshal Tito, and Ngo Dinh Diem all set up such courts.) In some countries treason is the name applied by politicians to the tactics of their rivals in a power struggle. The label of traitor sticks only to the losers.

Irish history is full of revolutionists condemned as traitors by English judges in English courts but who were exalted to the status of patriot martyrs when Ireland finally won her freedom from England. Today's Eire considers as traitors only those Irishmen who remained loyal to the British Government during the Irish uprisings.

When the Nazis occupied Norway, their Norwegian puppet,

Major Vidkun Quisling, arrested as traitors all of his country-men who sabotaged the German occupying forces. But after the war Quisling was executed by his fellow Norwegians for high treason. Similarly, French Premier Pierre Laval punished opposition to the German war effort as an act of treason to the Vichy Government. After the war the de Gaulle Government sentenced Laval to the firing squad as a traitor to France.

Secession poses baffling questions of treason. Were the Biafrans who felt oppressed and revolted against Nigeria traitors? Was it treason for an outraged South to secede from an abolitionist-minded North? Are we dealing with traitors or patriots in the Puerto Rican Revolutionary Armed Independence Movement, which in 1969 bombed American hotels on their island, seized a radio station, and called on all Puerto Ricans to join "patriots in a revolution against Yankee imperialism"?

Are we on solid moral ground to insist that our Government is *always* right ("Our country, right or wrong!") and that those citizens who disagree are traitors to the nation?

This book attempts the difficult task of exploring what is or is not treason, as illuminated by dramatic cases from American history. Baffling questions require answers:

Does the American Government have the right to use repressive measures to protect itself from overthrow? How far can it legally go—against whom and under what circumstances?

Is the Communist party, or any group dedicated to the overthrow of the Government, as entitled to advocate its policies as the Republican or Democratic parties?

Are Fascist groups that seek to turn the United States into a right-wing dictatorship, in the style of Hitler, Mussolini, and Franco, superpatriots or supertraitors?

Are Americans of foreign ancestry disloyal for feeling and maintaining cultural ties to the country of their fathers?

What is the dividing line between dissent and disloyalty? Is it treason for Americans to oppose a war in which the United States is involved?

Should a minority be allowed to decide which laws of a majority they will obey as just and which they will disobey as unjust?

How should treason be judged and punished?

How can all of us strengthen the bonds of loyalty we feel toward each other as Americans and help to prevent the development of situations that create disloyalty?

In the final analysis, each new generation of Americans must decide for itself how much opposition to the Government is every American citizen's right and how much is unsafe for the security of the whole society.

This book suggests guidelines for reaching your own conclusions about disloyalty and dissent. With other Americans of your generation who agree with you, you are free to urge those views upon your representatives in Congress in order to redefine American duties and liberties for our own day.

2   "WE SHALL ALL HANG SEPARATELY"

In earliest times any threat to, or attack on, the state or head of state was punished as treason. A monarch or judicial tribunal decided just which acts of opposition were traitorous. It was far from unusual for the charge of treason to be made for the purpose of political punishment.

The most open-and-shut cases of treason were those in which a citizen or soldier was found to have been paid by an insurrectionist, or agent of a foreign power, to commit an act of treachery against sovereign or state.

Yet at least one great Roman monarch saw nothing wrong in wider loyalties than those prescribed by national boundaries.

"My city and country . . . is Rome," said Marcus Aurelius, the brilliant Roman emperor and Stoic philosopher, "but so far as I am a man, it is the world." Early Christians also subscribed to the brotherhood of man as a paramount patriotism that came before loyalty to Rome.

In ancient Rome treason usually involved only the military. Accused men were charged with bearing arms against the state; communicating with the enemy; betraying a citizen to the enemy; desertion; or surrender to the enemy. Torture was sometimes used to extract confessions, but men accused as traitors were seldom put to death unless they confessed or there were two or more witnesses to their guilt.

The Romans were apparently more interested in exposing treason than in punishing it. A condemned traitor was often allowed to flee the country before the date set for his execution. Banishment from the Rome he had betrayed seemed to many citizens a more appropriate punishment, and indeed a more terrible one, than death.

The scope of treason was vastly increased in the sixth century under Justinian, when Roman emperors were declared divine. The Justinian Code, the basis for all later Western law, called it treason to question an emperor's choice of his successor; to plot the murder of high magistrates; to meet in a mob with weapons or stones; to set prisoners free illegally; to incite others to sedition; and to falsify public documents.

The intention was considered equivalent to the actual deed if either could be proved. A convicted traitor was stripped of his property and beheaded.

Under King Edward III, England basically adopted the Justinian concept of treason. The Treason Act of 1351 provided death for "high treason," defined as offenses against the Crown. Lesser penalties were prescribed for "petty treason"—offenses against private "superiors," such as disloyalty of wife to husband, servant to master. Petty treason later became defined as the crime of murder.

Today's British law still retains four early definitions of high treason: plotting or even "imagining" the death of any member of the royal family, having illegal sex relations with any female member of the royal family, levying war against the king, giving aid and comfort to his enemies.

It was left "in the breast of the judges to determine what was treason, or not so." The looseness with which the Statute of Treasons was often applied is exemplified in the fifteenth-century case of Walter Walker, who lived at a Cheapside inn called the Sign of the Crown.

Walker was overheard telling his little son that if he would be a good boy and go to sleep, his father would make him heir to the Crown—meaning the inn at which they were living. Arrested and accused of sinister intentions against the royal family, he was executed as a traitor.

During the reigns of Queen Anne and King George III, new definitions of treason were specified: attempting to prevent the king's chosen successor from coming to the throne and plotting to harm or kill the king and his heirs.

The earliest British penalties prescribed for a convicted traitor were barbaric. He was dragged to the place of execution by a horse, hung long enough to agonize him, cut down, disembowelled, then beheaded. Afterward his body was cut into quarters and "disposed of as the King might see fit."

Women found guilty of treason were often burned alive until 1790, after which they were usually beheaded or hanged. In 1848 most acts once branded as high treason were reduced to "treason felony," for which a convicted traitor could be sentenced to prison for anywhere from five years to life.

In the American colonies, as hostility deepened toward the Crown, colonists uneasily demanded that the scope of treason be limited only to levying war against the king or giving aid and comfort to his enemies. But King George III preferred the broad English law that left the power to determine what acts of opposition or dissent were treason in royal hands.

One of the earliest Americans charged with treason to the Crown was Nathaniel Bacon, a young Virginia plantation owner and member of the Governor's Council. He was indignant at the high-handed rule of Governor William Berkeley, especially at Berkeley's refusal to take action against Indian raids on border settlements.

Arming three hundred followers, Bacon led an authorized attack on Indians in 1676, slaughtering 150 red men. Governor Berkeley angrily charged him with treason and ordered his arrest. Bacon attacked and burned Jamestown, the capitol, putting Berkeley and the colonial Government to flight. British troop reinforcements were rushed to Virginia. The rebellion collapsed with Bacon's death from malaria. Berkeley vindictively ignored pardons for Bacon's followers signed by the king and hanged twenty-three of them as traitors to the Crown. He was ordered back to England but died before he had to answer for his own insubordination.

As the colonists grew increasingly dissatisfied with British rule, defiance bordering on treason became highly popular and was considered evidence of personal courage. Patrick Henry, a struggling, twenty-seven-year-old Virginia lawyer, won fame and clients in 1763 by a speech attacking the king's right to set aside laws passed by the popularly elected assemblies.

Pleading a case, Henry cried, "A king by annulling . . . laws of this salutary nature . . . forfeits all rights to his subjects' obedience!" Shocked cries rose in the courtroom: "Treason! Treason!" But his challenge to Crown arrogance proved so popular that he was elected to the Virginia legislature. In 1765 Henry authored the Virginia Resolutions, defying Britain's Stamp Act and reasserting the right of the colonies to legislate for themselves.

"Caesar had his Brutus," Henry told the legislature, "Charles the First his Cromwell, and George the Third——"

Again cries of "Treason! Treason! *Treason!*"

"—George the Third," he finished defiantly, "may profit by their example! If *this* be treason, make the most of it!"

Defiance of the Crown grew increasingly common in the decade preceding the American Revolution. King George III and Parliament, as well as the royal governors of the colonies, strove desperately to turn back the mounting tide of rebellion. Sometimes they appeased the colonists, sometimes they took a firm stand, and sometimes they punished them. But there were few arrests for treason, for fear of provoking an uprising.

American dissenters had some staunch supporters in the British Parliament itself, men such as Isaac Barré, for whom Barre, Vermont, was later named. Barré fondly called them "Sons of Liberty," a name adopted by colonial firebrands Samuel Adams and Paul Revere for a secret society they organized in the summer of 1765. The Sons sabotaged the unpopular Stamp Act, then went on to organize a boycott of British imports and spur the colonies to cooperate in fighting for self-government.

The result was the Stamp Act Congress that condemned taxation without representation and declared the Stamp Act illegal. American leaders in the colonial assemblies passed bills refusing to pay for troops quartered upon them or to collect royal taxes. The British Parliament angrily dissolved the New York and Massachusetts legislatures, calling them seditious. But no arrests were made.

The Sons of Liberty organized mob clashes with British troops in New York and Boston in 1770. The Boston riot was exaggerated and exploited by Sam Adams and Paul Revere as the "Boston Massacre" to stir revolutionary fervor throughout the colonies. Sam Adams organized the Committees of Correspondence to keep the colonies in touch with each other about new "outrages" by British authorities and to report measures of resistance taken by the colonies affected.

In February, 1772, the Boston assembly threatened secession from Britain unless the rights of the colonies were respected. That June eight boatloads of Sons of Liberty from Providence boarded the British customs schooner *Gaspee,* which had run aground at Namquit Point. Putting its officer and crew ashore, they set the schooner afire. Despite huge reward offers, only one witness could be found to accuse anyone, and his testimony was so contradictory as to be worthless.

The *Gaspee* incident clearly indicated to Parliament the extent of popular support enjoyed by American "traitors."

England was kept informed of treasonous moves in the colonies by Dr. Benjamin Church, chief surgeon of Washington's army, an informer who succeeded in winning a place on the twenty-one-man executive board of the Committees of Correspondence. It thus came as no surprise to the British when the tax imposed by Parliament's Tea Act resulted in a boycott of British tea.

But Church didn't find out until the British did that Sam Adams had sent Sons of Liberty disguised as Mohawk Indians to raid tea ships in Boston Harbor and dump their cargoes overboard. The Boston Tea Party provoked a stormy debate in Parliament.

Many members demanded that known leaders of the Sons such as Sam Adams, Paul Revere, and Patrick Henry be arrested and brought to England to stand trial for treason. Some insisted that entire colonies, which obviously supported these acts of defiance, be drastically punished. King George agreed with this latter view as the only way to teach the Americans a lesson.

Ignoring pleas by Chatham and Edmund Burke for a conciliatory policy, Parliament passed the Boston Port Act. Boston Harbor would be blockaded until Bostonians made restitution for the losses suffered by the East India Tea Company because of "dangerous commotions and insurrections." Further punitive laws were also decreed by the royal governor of Massachusetts.

Colonial indignation exploded. Only Georgia failed to send a representative to the first Continental Congress of thirteen colonies that met at Philadelphia in September, 1774. The Congress voted to boycott all British goods until Parliament agreed to give Americans a voice in their own affairs.

By April, 1775, colonial treason had gone so far that a New England militia was organized to resist British troops sent to enforce Parliament's decrees. The colonial guerrillas at Lexington and Concord "fired the shot heard round the world." One month later Benedict Arnold was authorized to raise a force to attack Fort Ticonderoga on Lake Champlain in order to capture armaments needed to resist the British Army.

The American Revolution had begun. In June, two days before the disastrous rout at Bunker Hill, George Washington was appointed commander in chief of the American forces.

Now, suddenly, the awkward decision about treason could no longer be avoided. Who were the traitors in the colonies—those disloyal to the British Crown or those disloyal to the American insurrection? On June 30, 1775, the Continental Congress passed the Articles of War, governing the conduct of soldiers enlisted in the rebellious Continental Army. Articles 5 and 6 authorized the punishment of any "mutiny and sedition" against the Revolution.

In August, King George III issued a Proclamation of Rebellion condemning the North American colonies for "traitorously preparing, ordering and levying war against us." Accusing many Englishmen in London of having carried on a "traitorous correspondence" with the rebels, the king forbade any further commerce with Americans guilty of "treasonable Commotions."

"I desire what is good," said George III; "therefore, everyone who does not agree with me is a traitor."

Toward the end of 1775 colonial leaders of the rebellion, who now called themselves patriots, began suspecting that Dr. Benjamin Church was the informer in their midst. Doubt became certainty when his mistress smuggled a coded letter through patriot lines to his brother-in-law in British-held Boston. Intercepted, it revealed that Church had been acting as a spy for British General Thomas B. Gage.

The Continental Congress, thunderstruck, ordered Church arrested as a traitor. He denied that he was guilty of treason since they were all still under British law, which defined treason as a betrayal of allegiance owed to the king. Baffled, Congress removed him from office, jailed him, then permitted him to leave the country. His ship was lost at sea.

At the insistence of the Revolutionary Army, Congress now passed a bill calling it treason, and prescribing the death penalty, for any American soldier to collaborate with the king's forces.

The new law was cited in June, 1776, when Thomas Hickey, a member of Washington's personal guard, unsuccessfully conspired to lead a force of patriots over to General William Howe's forces as they landed in New York. Washington court-martialed Hickey, who was hanged for "sedition and mutiny" and for holding a "treacherous correspondence with the enemy."

Washington told Congress that New York's mayor, David Mathews, had also been implicated in the plot. As a civilian, however, Mathews could not be prosecuted under the military-treason statute. The colonies, fighting for the right to self-government, were sensitive about giving Congress any federal power over civilians. So Congress simply passed a resolution stating that all colonists owed allegiance to the "United Colonies of America" and asking each colony to formulate its own laws punishing civilian traitors.

In January, 1776, as the fighting expanded from revolutionary resistance to a desperate full-scale civil war, Tom Paine called for a declaration of independence from Britain in his widely circulated pamphlet, *Common Sense*. Congress passed the Tory Act, requiring local patriots to explain the American cause to all Tories and to disarm any who refused to pledge fealty to the colonists. The word "traitor" was now applied to any American disloyal to the rebellion.

In British and American Tory eyes the Declaration of Independence, adopted on July 4, 1776, was the ultimate act of treason. When any people "suffer a long train of abuses and usurpations," declared the colonists, "it is their right, it is their duty to throw off such government."*

Having openly announced their treason to the British Crown, the Americans at Philadelphia were under no illusions about what would happen to them if their revolution failed.

"We must, indeed, all hang together," warned Benjamin Franklin, "or most assuredly we shall all hang separately."

It now became more important than ever to weed out from their midst those countrymen still loyal to the Crown.

---

* Almost two centuries later Americans were reminded of these words by the Smothers Brothers, who had been dropped from CBS-TV programming because of their anti-Establishment humor. In a special Washington's Birthday show on NBC-TV, they quoted from the Founding Fathers. "We want to show," explained Tom Smothers, "that these great men defended the rights of dissent and free speech, and that to criticize your government does not make you a traitor. It makes you a modern patriot."

3   TRAITORS AGAINST TREASON

Few voices denouncing treason to the Revolution were louder than that of Major General Charles Lee, a fire-eating professional soldier who had fought in the French and Indian War, married a Seneca chief's daughter, and campaigned with Washington.

When Howe's forces threatened New York in the autumn of 1776, Lee won Washington's permission to defend that sector and to deal harshly with the Tories of Long Island.

"Not to crush those Serpents," Lee warned, "before their rattles are grown, would be ruinous." He assured Congress that he would purge New York and its environs of traitors.

His troops raided the homes of suspected Tories, packing off prisoners to Connecticut. But when Howe took New York, forcing Washington to retreat across the Delaware, Lee was captured by a British patrol. Threatened with hanging, he saved his neck by promising Howe to betray Washington, a secret later revealed by British historians.

Unaware of Lee's defection, Washington ransomed him from

the British by freeing some Hessian officers. Lee, restored to his command while secretly pledged to work "sincerely and zealously" for a British victory, sabotaged his orders to engage British forces near Monmouth, New Jersey, in support of an attack by Washington. His order to his troops to retreat instead resulted in a court-martial for cowardice. Unsuspected of treason, he was simply removed from his command.

When he eventually died on his Virginia estate, he was buried with honor as "a great American soldier and patriot."

The British scrupulously distinguished between the acts of military spying and treason. When they caught twenty-four-year-old American Captain Nathan Hale, disguised as a schoolmaster, gathering military information behind their lines in Long Island, he was hanged as a spy. It was as an American patriot, rather than as a traitor to the Crown, however, that he was allowed to utter his famous last words, "I only regret that I have but one life to lose for my country."

In British eyes the real traitors were the civilian leaders of the Revolution. To negotiate a treaty with the Dutch in 1780, Congress sent Henry Laurens, the South Carolinian who had been President of the Continental Congress two years earlier. Captured at sea, he was brought to England and clapped in the Tower of London on charges of high treason.

The British offered to spare his life if he confessed that he was a traitor to the Crown and transferred his allegiance. Laurens defied his captors. He was no British traitor, he insisted, but an American civilian prisoner of war. Two years later he was finally exchanged for a celebrated British prisoner in America, Lord Cornwallis, in time to join Franklin, Jay, and John Adams in signing a preliminary peace treaty.

The most celebrated traitor of the American Revolution was, of course, Benedict Arnold. From 1775 to 1778 Arnold fought so bravely that he won promotions from captain to major general. Twice wounded, he was the last American anyone would have suspected of treachery. But Arnold was a vainglorious, overambitious man for whom honors and promotions never came soon enough or often enough.

He had constant run-ins with his superiors, who found him imperious and difficult to get along with. Appointed commander of Philadelphia in 1778, he rode into the city as a military hero but a social zero. Taking over the fine mansion Howe had vacated, Arnold set about making an impression socially on the city's elite by entertaining extravagantly.

Soon deep in debt, he paid off Tory creditors with political favors. He married eighteen-year-old blond Tory socialite Margaret Shippen, whose expensive tastes plunged him even more deeply into debt. In 1780 he was court-martialed because of charges brought by the Council of Philadelphia that he was abusing his military authority. Found guilty, he was sentenced to be reprimanded by General Washington.

Washington, who respected Arnold's military abilities, rebuked him mildly. The proud Arnold was outraged by his humiliation at the hands of fellow citizens who, he felt, owed him a debt of gratitude for his heroic services on their behalf.

He was still brooding when his wife, Peggy, showed him a letter from British Major John André, an old beau of hers from the days of the British occupation of Philadelphia. André was now with Howe's forces in New York, serving as adjutant general to General Henry Clinton. The letter offered Peggy's husband twenty thousand pounds if he could obtain command of West Point and turn it over to the British. Arnold could also expect a high command with Howe's forces if he succeeded.

Still debt-ridden and bitter at his treatment, Arnold agreed to turn his coat. Washington offered him another field command, but Arnold pleaded that old wounds were bothering him and asked for the West Point command instead. When Washington consented, Arnold notified André at once. He also informed the British where Washington would be sleeping one night, but the information reached Clinton too late to be of use.

The British sloop *Vulture* brought André up the Hudson at night for a rendezvous with Arnold to arrange the surrender of West Point to the British. He was wearing a British uniform, but daybreak made it advisable for him to get back to the *Vulture* in civilian clothes with a pass signed by Arnold.

As he went through the American lines, his aristocratic manner made three American militiamen suspicious. They turned him over to their lieutenant as a possible spy with a forged pass. The lieutenant suspected that André was someone important because of wig powder in his hair, and notified Major Benjamin Tallmadge, of the new American Secret Service.

Tallmadge notified Washington, who was preparing to visit West Point. Word also reached Arnold that André had been taken. Arnold at once fled for refuge aboard the *Vulture,* lying in the Hudson, only hours before Washington reached his house for a breakfast appointment. Washington was confused by Arnold's mysterious absence, but all became clear when papers found in Major André's boot were rushed to him. He at once set about strengthening the sabotaged defenses of West Point.

On September 26, 1780, General Nathaniel Greene grimly issued general orders to the American troops, revealing to them that they had been betrayed by a top commander:

> *Treason* of the blackest dye was yesterday discovered! General Arnold, who commanded at West Point, lost to every sentiment of honor, of public and private obligation, was about to deliver up that important post into the hands of the enemy. Such an event must have given the American cause a deadly wound, if not a fatal stab. Happily, the

treason has been timely discovered. . . . Great honor is due to the American Army that this is the first instance of treason of the kind.

André asked to be shot, as that was a suitable military execution, but was sent to the gallows instead, where he coolly fixed the noose around his own neck. The British paid Arnold £6,315 for his unsuccessful treachery and gave him a field commission as a brigadier general. He fought against the Continental Army at Richmond, Virginia, and burned New London, Connecticut, massacring the defenders of Fort Griswold when they surrendered. British officers loathed him as an "ungentlemanly brute and traitor."

"General Arnold is a very unpopular character in the British army," observed the London *Lloyd's Evening Post* on October 11, 1780, "nor can all the patronage he meets with from the commander-in-chief procure him respectability. . . . The subaltern officers have conceived such an aversion to him, that they unanimously refused to serve under his command."

When the war was over Arnold sought to cling to his British commission, but the British had had enough of him. In 1783 he went to New Brunswick, Canada, where he became a merchant in the West Indies trade. Four years later accusations of dishonesty drove him to London, where war had broken out with France. He sought to fit out privateers, but was so shunned and despised that he suffered what amounted to a nervous breakdown. He literally welcomed death on June 14, 1801, less than two months after the inauguration of a new Vice President of the United States who would soon rival Arnold in popular infamy as a celebrated traitor—Aaron Burr.

Americans were shocked when another Revolutionary hero was also revealed to be engaged in treasonable intercourse with the enemy. Connecticut-born Ethan Allen had moved in 1769 to that part of the New Hampshire Grants that became Vermont. The New York legislature charged that many settlers in western Vermont were actually on the New York side of the border, and insisted they must repurchase their property from Albany.

Indignant, Ethan Allen and his younger brother, Ira, organized the Green Mountain Boys, sworn to resist any attempt to drive Vermonters off their lands. The quarrel was momentarily forgotten with the outbreak of the Revolution. Allen became a hero when he led his Green Mountain Boys, under Benedict Arnold, to capture Fort Ticonderoga in May, 1775. He also won fame as a rough, fearless leader in expeditions against Canada under Schuyler and Montgomery.

The British finally captured him near Montreal in September, 1775. Imprisoned for two and a half years, Allen was released in an exchange of prisoners in May, 1778, after Washington warned that if he were executed for treason, the Americans would execute British prisoners as traitors.

A grateful Congress brevetted Allen colonel in the Continental Army and a major general in the militia. He returned home to the New Hampshire Grants, where his brother Ira had led a movement that broke away their section as the separate state of Vermont.

But congressional opposition blocked recognition of Vermont as a state. Ethan Allen angrily decided that if the United States could secede from Britain to win independence, then Vermont could secede from the United States for exactly the same reason.

Entering negotiations with Sir Frederick Haldimand, Governor General of Canada, Allen proposed making Vermont a Canadian province. He warned Congress bluntly in March, 1781, "I am as resolutely determined to defend the independence of Vermont as Congress that of the United States, and rather than fail will retire with the hardy Green Mountain Boys into the desolate caverns of the mountains and wage war."

Furious congressmen demanded Allen's arrest for treason. But cooler heads prevailed, suggesting that his dealings with Sir Frederick and his defiance of Congress were not intended as treachery, but only as pressure upon the Congress.

On March 4, 1791, after Ethan Allen had died at Burlington, his "constructive treason" was restored to the columns of patriotism by Vermont's admission to statehood.

It was not until fully two years after the Declaration of Independence that Americans had a national definition of treason. Until then treason had been a matter for each state to deal with separately. When the Constitution was ratified on September 13, 1788, the crime of treason—the only crime defined in the Constitution—was finally spelled out. Article III, Section 3, declared:

> Treason against the United States shall consist only in levying war against them, or in adhering to their enemies, giving them aid and comfort. No person shall be convicted of treason unless on the testimony of two witnesses to the same overt act, or on confession in open court. The Congress shall have power to declare the punishment of treason, but no attainder [deprivation of civil and legal rights] of treason shall work corruption of blood, or forfeiture except during the life of the person attained.

The attainder clause was intended to prevent extension of punishment to a traitor's heirs. "Levying war" has been construed by Constitutional authorities to mean defiance of the Government by armed force but more than just rioting or interfering with execution of the law. "Adhering to their enemies, giving them aid and comfort," has been interpreted as giving material assistance, voluntarily, to countries with which the United States is at war.

The First Congress, meeting on March 4, 1789, set the

penalty for treason as death or imprisonment and fine, at the discretion of the court. The minimum penalty was five years' imprisonment, a ten-thousand-dollar fine, and inability to hold public office. An alien temporarily residing in the United States may be as guilty of treason as a citizen, on the theory that he owes a duty of allegiance to the country because he is sheltered under the protection of its laws while he is here.

In 1790 Congress decreed that the penalty for treason would be death by hanging. An accused person had to be given a copy of the indictment and a list of witnesses and jurors at least three days before trial. He was guaranteed counsel and the right to challenge thirty-five selections for the jury panel. If he chose to be mute at the trial, he would be considered as having entered a plea of "not guilty."

The treason clause did not become national law until after the war because otherwise it would have been necessary for the Government to execute or imprison up to two hundred thousand Loyalists. Instead they went into exile, forcibly or voluntarily.

Unlike the bloodthirsty leaders of the French Revolution, American Revolution leaders were reluctant to execute fellow citizens who had aided the British or opposed the Revolution. Many of the Founding Fathers themselves had not reached the decision to be disloyal to the Crown without great anguish.

John Adams later confessed that he would have given anything he owned during the Revolution if somehow it could have been magically erased and the old colonial system restored. Relatives of Washington, Franklin, John and Sam Adams remained loyal to the Crown. In many families there were similar divisions between father and son, brother and brother.

Understandably, many states preferred to pardon acts of treason by "acts of grace" when apprehended Loyalists agreed to take an oath of allegiance to the United States. Likewise, many British leaders were equally loath to regard the Americans in arms against them as guilty of treason.

"We do not call you rebels or traitors," Edmund Burke had told them from Parliament in January, 1777. "We do not call for the vengeance of the Crown against you. . . . On the contrary, we highly revere the principles on which you act, though we lament some of their effects."

Disloyalty to the new Republic was sometimes inspired less by allegiance to the Crown than by simple war-weariness. After four years of a revolt that had bled the country white of men, money, and goods, there was widespread unrest not only among the troops, many of whom were deserting, but also among the civilian population.

In Virginia, attempts to draft more men for Washington led to statewide riots. One riot leader, John Claypole, of Hampshire County, defied the sheriff, cursed Congress, and drank a public toast to the king. He and forty-one other rioters were arrested by state militia and charged with treason. But all were pardoned when the court selected to try them failed to convene because the commissioners prudently neglected to arrive.

At the end of the war the treason law took on a different coloration because of the new Republic's problems. Now it was no longer a question of allegiance to an external enemy but of rebellion against the authority of a weak new government. The Federalists in power were extremely sensitive to criticism and saw opposition to government edicts as the forerunner of treason, if not treason itself.

Shays' Rebellion in Massachusetts in 1786 was the first major armed insurrection that sought to prevent the enforcement of federal laws. After the war poor farmers were stripped of their farms, cattle, and possessions for inability to pay heavy taxes and debts. Many were thrown into debtors' prison by the wealthy merchants of Boston and Salem who controlled the Massachusetts legislature.

Mobs of farmers prevented courts from sitting so that no judgments could be passed against them. Issuing a proclamation against unlawful assemblies, Governor James Bowdoin called out the militia in September, 1786. The Regulators, as the poor farmers called themselves, elected war hero Daniel Shays as their leader. Shays, too, was in trouble because he could not pay a twelve-dollar debt. He led 1,100 men in shutting down the State Supreme Court at Springfield, which was preparing to indict him and other leading Regulators for treason.

After freeing imprisoned debtors, they sought to raid the federal arsenal for arms. But militia led by Major General Shepherd scattered them with artillery, killing four. Later a force led by General Benjamin Lincoln pursued them through the countryside. Shays escaped to Vermont, but fourteen of his followers were caught and sentenced to die as traitors.

A storm of public protest, however, forced the authorities to pardon some Regulators and let others off with short prison terms. Indignation swept the old legislature out of office. The new one granted some of the Regulators' demands and permitted Shays to return home.

Washington and his Federalists were deeply worried about the explosive instability of the new Republic. The same oppressive conditions of the poor that had provoked Shays' Rebellion existed in all states of the Union. Thomas Jefferson, now American minister to France, was certainly not helping matters by declaring cheerfully from Paris: "A little rebellion now and then is a good thing; the tree of liberty must be refreshed from time to time with the blood of patriots and tyrants." Did *all* governments, indeed, become tyrannies?

Was permanent treason the obligation of patriots?

4

THE INCREDIBLE AARON BURR

The apprehension of the Federalists was intensified one year after Jefferson resigned from Washington's Cabinet to organize an opposition to Alexander Hamilton's policies. Hamilton saw Jefferson's influence in the outbreak of the Whiskey Rebellion.

When Hamilton had passed an excise tax on whiskey-making in 1791, Jefferson had predicted that it would be defied as "odious" by backwoods Scotch-Irish farmers of the Monongahela Valley in western Pennsylvania. They depended upon marketing their grain in the form of more easily transportable whiskey. Every farm had its own distillery. The tax was unwise, Jefferson warned, because collecting it would commit "the authority of the government in parts where resistance is most probable and coercion less practicable."

His predictions proved accurate. The whiskey farmers, viewing the tax as just as oppressive as the British Stamp Tax had been to all Americans, organized to resist it. Distillers who paid it were threatened. Revenue officers who entered Monongahela Valley were driven off bodily.

Washington and Hamilton angrily insisted that Pennsylvania Governor Thomas Mifflin put down the insurrection. A Jeffersonian Republican, he refused. If anyone was going to be unpopular for using force against the whiskey farmers, let it be the Federalists. It was *their* law!

Hamilton warned the President that federal power and determination were being tested. If the Government did not act vigorously to enforce the laws of Congress, then state power would be recognized as paramount. Americans in any state would be free to defy any federal laws they opposed.

Convinced, on August 7, 1794, Washington called out and federalized fifteen thousand militia troops from Virginia, Maryland, and Pennsylvania. This army was led across the Alleghenies by Generals Daniel Morgan and Henry Lee, accompanied by Alexander Hamilton in uniform. It was an absurdly large force to put down some regional rioting—as large as the army that had captured Cornwallis. But it suited Hamilton's purpose to demonstrate the great power of the Federal Government.

The whiskey rebels fled and the disorders were quickly quelled. Hamilton ordered eighteen farmers seized for trial in Philadelphia as traitors. Only two were convicted, however, and Washington pardoned both when it became embarrassingly apparent that raising an army against the desperate farmers of western Pennsylvania had been a serious political mistake.

There was widespread indignation against the Federalists in power for this flexing of military might against the people. The Jeffersonians soared in popularity as a new "party of the people" opposed to an aristocratic federal bureaucracy.

When Adams succeeded Washington as President in 1797, it was not lost on him that Jefferson, as his closest rival, had been elected Vice President. Adams had to respect Jefferson's views on what to do about French interference with American shipping during the Franco-British war. Hawk Federalists in the

Cabinet demanded war against France, but Jefferson's Republicans were vehemently opposed.

Adams discreetly compromised. He ordered strong defense measures but left the decision for war or peace up to the French. An undeclared naval war began in July, 1798. Hamilton increased his pressure on Adams for a declaration of war. He was infuriated by opposition from French-speaking Americans, considering them traitors. The Federalists also worried about the voting power of Irish immigrants, who were likewise flocking into Jefferson's Republican party.

Hamilton finally prevailed upon Adams to act against "treasonable activities against the United States" by sponsoring the Alien and Sedition Acts of 1798. On June 18 the Naturalization Act blocked immigrants from exercising their vote by requiring fourteen, rather than five, years of residence for citizenship. One week later the Alien Act authorized the President to deport all aliens suspected of "treasonable or secret" activities.

Two weeks later the Alien Enemies Act authorized the President, upon declaration of war, to arrest, imprison, or deport aliens still citizens of the enemy power. The following week the Sedition Act imposed fines and imprisonment on any citizens or aliens who participated in "any insurrection, riot, unlawful assembly, or combination." Anyone convicted of publishing "false, scandalous, and malicious writing" was subject to a fine of up to two thousand dollars and two years in jail.

Vigorously enforced by the Federalists to destroy Jefferson's Republican party, the new laws branded all political opposition as treason. Some twenty-five leading Americans, all Jeffersonians, were arrested, and ten were convicted, including one member of Congress.

Lyon Matthew, an Irish immigrant who edited a paper called *The Scourge of Aristocracy,* denounced President Adams as a bully. Arrested in Vermont, he was fined one thousand dollars and sentenced to four months in a miserable dungeon. The Green Mountain Boys rallied to his cause, forwarding petitions signed by thousands of Vermonters to Adams, who spurned them.

Indignant Vermont Republicans paid Matthew's fine and ran him for Congress. Elected by an overwhelming majority, he was sent to Washington in a sleigh at the head of a twelve-mile procession of jubilant Jeffersonians.

In Kentucky, Jefferson took the lead in passing state resolutions branding the Alien and Sedition Acts unconstitutional, while in Virginia James Madison did the same. The laws were defied by a new uprising in February, 1799, against a federal property-tax levied by Hamilton to raise money for the war he was confident of inciting against France.

Tax collectors who went into Pennsylvania Dutch regions were forced to duck hot water poured on them from upper farmhouse windows by farmers' wives. When marshals arrested some of the farmers, seven hundred men led by former Continental Army officer John Fries forced their release. They drove the marshals off, crying, *"Dämm de President, dämm de Congress, dämm de Arischdokratz!"* Ironically, John Fries had been an ardent supporter of John Adams.

The President, calling a Cabinet meeting, issued an angry proclamation against "certain acts, which, I am advised, amount to treason, being overt acts of levying war against the United States." A cavalry and artillery force of two thousand militia from New Jersey was dispatched in a new show of federal force. Fries was seized, tried for treason, and sentenced to hang.

He won a retrial when his lawyers proved that one of the jurors had concealed prejudice against him. But they withdrew from his defense when a second trial before "hanging judge" Samuel Chase, of Philadelphia, made it impossible for them to defend him fairly. Condemned again, Fries begged the President to spare him. But the Federalist Cabinet unanimously insisted that he must hang as an example.

Adams, an austere man but not without conscience, felt that martyring Fries was not only unjust but likely to provoke more revolts. Knowing his action would infuriate Hamilton and split the Federalist party seriously, he nevertheless insisted upon pardoning Fries. His courage shattered Federalist unity, letting the Jeffersonians win the White House. The Jeffersonians quickly saw to it that the repressive Alien and Sedition Acts were rendered inoperative.

"I discharged every person under punishment or prosecution under the sedition law," Jefferson said, "because I considered . . . that law to be a nullity, as absolute and palpable as if Congress had ordered us to fall down and worship a golden image."

In December, 1801, when Republicans Jefferson and Aaron Burr were tied for the Presidency in electoral votes, the House of Representatives decided in Jefferson's favor. The crucial vote was cast by Hamilton, who hated Jefferson but loathed Burr.

The brilliant, witty, and charming Aaron Burr was bitterly disappointed at being nosed out of the Presidency. Driven by an all-consuming hunger for power, he was galled at having to serve in Jefferson's shadow. Jefferson, in turn, soon found himself irked by Burr's disloyalty to the Republican party.

In January, 1802, Burr broke a tie vote in the Senate to vote with the Federalists in defeating an important Republican judiciary-reform bill that Jefferson wanted. Weeks later Burr was the sole Republican attending a Federalist dinner, at which he proposed a toast to "the union of all honest men." Burr's flirtation with the Federalists was unmistakable; he wanted their nomination to oppose Jefferson's reelection. Jefferson privately called Burr "a crooked gun . . . whose aim or shot you could never be sure of."

When Jefferson purchased the Louisiana Territory in 1803, Federalist leaders in New England assembled in a secret conclave called the Essex Junto. They were afraid that the Louisiana Territory would give southern agrarian states a balance of power over New England's manufacturing states.

Led by Adams's former Secretary of State, Timothy Pickering, of Massachusetts, the Essex Junto plotted a secession of New England, New York, and New Jersey from the Union. The conspiracy called for establishing, with British support, a northern confederacy "exempt from the corrupt and corrupting influence and oppression of the aristocratic democrats of the South." British minister Anthony Merry pledged cooperation.

Control of New York was vital to the plot. The Essex Junto sought Alexander Hamilton as their candidate on the Federalist ticket for governor, but he spurned their conspiracy. So Pickering offered the role to Burr, whom Jefferson was dropping from the Republican ticket in the presidential elections of 1800. Burr promptly accepted.

He lost the campaign after bitter opposition to him by Hamilton as "a dangerous man, and one who ought not to be trusted with the reins of government." Once more Hamilton's enmity had frustrated Burr's ambitions. His political career wrecked, Burr forced Hamilton into a duel and killed him. Public indignation was so great that Burr was indicted for murder in New Jersey and felt compelled to flee.

During his last days as Vice President, Burr had made a desperate offer to British minister Anthony Merry to split the Louisiana Territory from the Union and put it under the Union Jack. The price he asked was $500,000 and the loan of a British naval force. Merry relayed the offer to London, but the British Foreign Office considered Burr a lost, and extremely unreliable, cause.

Debt-ridden from living beyond his means, his reputation ruined on the eastern seaboard, Aaron Burr conceived a daring plan to retrieve his fortunes. The Louisiana Territory and

Spanish Mexico were poorly defended lands. Why not turn land pirate, seize them with a private army, and proclaim himself emperor? He could then induce the vast Mississippi Territory to join him and so would rule an empire far greater and richer than Jefferson's miserable little seaboard republic!

Major General James Wilkinson, an old war comrade who was now commander in chief of the U.S. Army as well as governor of the Louisiana Territory, was induced to support Burr's conspiracy. Like Burr an unscrupulous opportunist, Wilkinson was even on Spain's payroll as a secret agent. He supplied the former Vice President with a military escort and a houseboat equipped with sails to take him down the Mississippi.

Among the influential Americans Burr solicited for support was Andrew Jackson, who at first cooperated under the impression that war with Spain was imminent and that Burr had been secretly authorized by the White House to organize a filibustering expedition to seize the Floridas.

Harman Blennerhasset, a wealthy Irish landowner, was thrilled with Burr's offer to make him Grand Chamberlain of the proposed empire and became an ardent supporter. By 1806 they had recruited a small private army of adventurers, assembling them on ten flatboats in Kentucky's Cumberland River.

Joseph H. Daveiss, U.S. district attorney for Kentucky, accused Burr of seeking to mount an unauthorized expedition against Mexico. Burr brazenly confronted him in Frankfort, demanding that he prove the charge. Twice Daveiss empaneled a grand jury; twice Burr was acquitted for lack of evidence.

Jefferson observed these developments from Washington in worried silence. Many Americans thought that the silence from the White House meant that Burr was acting with the President's knowledge and secret consent, a notion Burr's hints encouraged. But Jefferson finally sent an emissary to the governors of Ohio and Kentucky to urge seizure of Burr's flotilla.

A worried General Wilkinson reached the conclusion that Burr's flamboyant venture was doomed to failure. Deciding not to risk swinging beside Burr for treason, he covered his tracks by writing a letter to Jefferson revealing his old friend's "deep, dark, wicked, and widespread conspiracy."

Burr, he warned, was planning to seize New Orleans, plunder bank funds, take over the arsenal and military stores, then raid Mexico. The buccaneer was also spreading the impression that his schemes were secretly endorsed by the Federal Government. Wilkinson had gone to New Orleans, Jefferson was assured, to marshal the city's defenses against Burr's treachery.

By this time all kinds of wild rumors were agitating Congress, which demanded that the President reveal what was going on. Jefferson sent them word on January 22, 1807, that "an illegal combination of private individuals against the peace and safety of the Union, and a military expedition" against Mexico had been uncovered. The traitor responsible, Jefferson revealed, was Aaron Burr, whose "guilt is placed beyond question."

Announcing a reward for Burr's arrest, Jefferson praised General Wilkinson for his patriotic exposé of the former Vice President. The news reached Burr in Mississippi. He at once fled on horseback, disguised as a backwoodsman. Even more than the bounty-hunters, Burr feared the military escort Wilkinson had given him, dreading that the commander in chief would order him killed to seal his lips about Wilkinson's complicity.

Burr was captured in Alabama and brought to Richmond, Virginia, to stand trial on two counts—high treason against the United States and a high misdemeanor for plotting the Mexican invasion. William Eaton, a former American consul, testified that Burr had confided to him the plot to set up a midwest empire with its capital in New Orleans, from which Mexico would be added by conquest. Wilkinson was to overthrow the Government with the Army, assassinate Jefferson, and add the eastern states to Burr's new empire. Eaton further testified that he had warned the President, who had refused to believe Burr and Wilkinson would betray their country.

Burr, a lawyer, joined the defense as his own counsel. He accused Wilkinson of having frightened the President into alarming the American people. There was not a shred of evidence, he insisted, other than the affidavits of Wilkinson and Eaton, which were "abounding in crudities and absurdities."

The arraignment was held before Chief Justice John Marshall, sitting in Richmond, Virginia. Marshall found grounds for a charge of high misdemeanor in the matter of planning to invade Mexico but questioned the evidence for a charge of high treason. The prosecution had failed to produce the two witnesses required by the Constitution to testify to Burr's assemblage of forces to levy war on the United States.

Jefferson expressed doubts about the impartiality of Marshall, who disliked the President as much as Jefferson disliked him. Had not Marshall even attended a dinner with Burr at the home of Burr's defense counsel, John Wickham, while waiting for the trial to begin? Another Burr lawyer, Virginia's Edmund Randolph, argued that the prosecution had simply not proved the use of force against the Government or even the intent to commit treason. Burr's trial, Randolph charged, was political persecution.

Justice Marshall cautioned the jury that Burr had to be given the full benefit of his constitutional rights before he could be found guilty of treason. The jury found Burr not guilty "by any evidence submitted to us."

He was then tried for a high misdemeanor—violating the 1794 Act of Congress forbidding any American to mount a military expedition against a country with which the United States was at peace.

Once again Marshall warned that the jury must accept only

the strictest legal evidence, with the benefit of the doubt properly belonging to Burr. The jury took only half an hour to return another not-guilty verdict. General Wilkinson indignantly protested to Jefferson that Burr's acquittal was nothing less than the work of a "corrupt judge."

"The scenes which have been acting at Richmond," Jefferson wrote gloomily to a close friend, "are sufficient to fill us with alarm. We supposed we possessed fixed laws to guard us equally against treason and oppression; but it now appears we have no law but the will of the judge."

Despite his belated return to loyalty, Wilkinson did not escape arraignment before a grand jury for "misprision of treason"— the hiding of a crime by one who knows about it. But by a narrow vote of 9 to 7, his initial lapse of patriotism was not prosecuted. The grand jury was not allowed to know that during the Revolution Wilkinson had also been a conspirator in the Conway Cabal, an unsuccessful intrigue to overthrow Washington and replace him with General Horatio Gates.

Although two juries had acquitted Burr of the charges against him, most Americans were convinced with Jefferson that he had indeed been a traitor. Later revelations in the 1890s from British and Spanish archives bore out this conviction.

British minister Anthony Merry's reports revealed that Burr, driven by ambition and spite toward Jefferson, had asked the British for £100,000 to finance an army that would seize Louisiana and the American West for the British flag. The British had ignored him as a flamboyant and irresponsible adventurer.

Spanish minister Marquis de Casa Yrujo's reports revealed that Burr had sent an emissary, New Jersey Senator Jonathan Dayton, to ask forty thousand dollars for vital information involving Spanish interests. Dayton had revealed to Casa Yrujo the Burr plot to seize the Spanish Floridas and Mexico, capture the White House, imprison Jefferson, and plunder the U.S. Treasury.

Had their respective governments permitted Merry and Casa Yrujo to testify at the treason trials, it is quite likely that Burr would have been hanged as a traitor. Freed instead under a cloud of suspicion, he fled to Europe in 1808. For four years he vainly sought to interest the British Parliament in his wild schemes. The scornful British finally lost patience and ordered him out of the country, as contemptuous of his treason as they had been of Benedict Arnold's.

Nearly destitute, Burr borrowed money from loyal friends and wandered disconsolately through Europe in search of a government willing to back his military fantasies. All monarchs, including Napoleon, scorned his powerless promises. Dejected, Burr tried to return home but was refused a passport by the American ministry in Paris—the Jefferson influence exerted through the Madison Administration.

The outbreak of war with Britain in 1812, however, softened the American memory of Burr's treachery, and he was permitted to return to New York City. Giving up all schemes for power and glory, Burr prudently set himself a more practical goal— marriage to the rich widow Jumel. When he died at the age of eighty in 1836, Burr left many believers still convinced that he had been unjustly accused of treason.

5

"SHOWERS
OF BLOOD"

The prelude to the War of 1812 was the outbreak of the Napoleonic wars that led both England and France to seek to control American shipping lanes for their own advantage. The Jeffersonians were forced to impose a series of Embargo Acts between 1807 and 1809 forbidding trade with any power refusing to respect American rights at sea. The acts were bitterly opposed by the mercantile Federalists of New England.

Timothy Pickering, who four years earlier had masterminded the unsuccessful Essex Junto plot, now threatened New England's secession once more. He assured British envoy George Rose that there would be no second war against England, because he, Pickering, would soon lead a new American revolution. As president of a New England confederation his first act would be to nullify the Embargo Acts and resume trade with England.

Pickering called upon the New England states to defy the Embargo Acts as unconstitutional. All Federalist leaders supported his proposal. New England legislatures and towns announced their refusal to cooperate in enforcing the acts; governors refused to furnish militia officers for enforcement. Pickering then proposed a New England convention to nullify the Embargo.

The arrest of Pickering and other Federalist leaders for high treason was demanded by infuriated Republicans in President Madison's Cabinet and by war hawks in Congress anxious to go to war with England to seize Canadian territory. But Madison, recalling the arrests of Republicans under the Alien and Sedition Acts, refused to persecute political opponents.

Pickering's drive for secession was restrained by the powerful leader of the Federalist party, George Cabot, who insisted that they wait until the strategic moment—the new war with Britain he foresaw. The Government would then be too involved with the foreign enemy to prevent the breakaway of an independent New England confederation.

On June 1, 1812, Madison asked Congress to declare war on Britain. New England (except Vermont), New York, New Jersey, and Delaware voted for peace, but the war hawks of the South and West prevailed.

Some conservative Republicans angrily supported Federalist opposition to "Mr. Madison's war." They forced an adjournment of Congress without voting a single bill to increase the tiny American Navy, which would now have to fight the world's greatest sea power.

"It is not the Federalists who are the party of treason," flared one indignant war hawk. "It is Madison's own party who are proving traitors to the nation in its hour of dire peril!"

The Federalists did everything they could to obstruct the war effort. The Massachusetts legislature, proposing the organization of a new peace party, urged citizens not to volunteer for a war "against the nation from which we are descended." Three New

England governors would not call the state militia into national service. Federalist merchants refused to buy war bonds or fit out privateers for the Government.

"Blue-light Federalists" actually signaled British blockaders offshore to alert them to the presence and impending attacks of American warships. Federalist newspapers spoke out against the war. Madison's own former Secretary of State, Robert Smith, attacked the war in a public speech. Chief Justice Marshall called it a "base submission of the United States to Napoleon's wishes."

Madison still refused to take action against such "aid and comfort to the enemy" by ordering arrests for treason. He dreaded splitting and polarizing the country more than it already was. Besides, how could he accuse Federalist leaders of treason for opposing the war, when they could quote his own attack on advocates of an enlarged military as treasonous? When Hamilton and the Federalists had sought to increase the standing army, Madison had found it monstrous "that the traitors should . . . pursue some fixed plan for the extension of the military establishment."

The case of the New England governors who refused to call up the state militia for federal service did not reach the Supreme Court until 1827. In *Martin v. Mott* the Court agreed with Madison that the President, acting under congressional authority, was sole judge of emergencies that required the calling up of state militia, and that his decision was binding on all state officials.*

But on December 15, 1815, when the British launched attacks on the Maine coast, there were no federal troops stationed on the New England seaboard to resist them. At Hartford twenty-six

---

* Whether it is equally binding in cases of undeclared wars such as Vietnam is still not clear. The Massachusetts legislature raised the question for the Supreme Court by passing a bill in April, 1970, holding it illegal to draft any citizen of Massachusetts for an American war that had not been declared by Congress.

delegates from New England states met behind locked doors in a secret convention to decide on steps for ending the war and the Embargo Acts.

A committee was dispatched to Washington to negotiate their demands. If those demands were rejected, Cabot hinted, the northern seaboard would consider Pickering's plan of seceding as a northern confederacy. But by the time the committee reached Washington, the country was celebrating Jackson's victory in New Orleans and the war was over.

The Federalist party was widely castigated for its role in sponsoring the Hartford convention. The Republicans accused Pickering, Cabot, and other Federalists of "conspiracy, sedition, and treason," but no arrests were made. The Federalist party was so discredited, however, that it did not survive the Presidential election of 1816 but eventually reemerged as the Whig party.

During the Tyler Administration (1841–45) the question of treason to a state government became a stormy issue.

When Rhode Island had been granted a charter by King Charles in 1663, it had restricted the vote to property owners and their eldest sons. In 1776 a majority of these Federalist agriculturists had simply adopted the charter as Rhode Island's state constitution. As the state gradually became industrialized, foreign-born workers who flocked into the cities—mostly Irish Catholics—found themselves voteless and at the mercy of the rural Protestant minority.

Thomas Wilson Dorr, a brilliant young lawyer who had been admitted to Harvard at the age of fourteen, published an *Address to the People of Rhode Island,* challenging the legality of the Whig state government. Although the American Revolution had severed all state ties to England, Dorr pointed out, Rhode Island had illegally continued to base its government on a British charter.

In October, 1841, a citizens' convention of Democrats under

his leadership framed a "People's Constitution" that gave voting rights to all adult white male citizens. The new constitution was overwhelmingly approved by fourteen thousand Rhode Islanders, who voted for it in extralegal gatherings.

Governor Samuel W. King immediately denounced the Democratic referendum as illegal. Confusion reigned over who now had the right to vote in Rhode Island elections. The King (Whig) and Dorr (Democratic) factions held separate elections for governor on April 18, 1842. Each side won its own election, and both claimed victory. King was reinaugurated at Newport. Dorr, whose strength was in the northwest, was inaugurated as governor in a Providence foundry.

King angrily rammed the Algerine Law through the legislature. This bill decreed all unauthorized public assemblages to be illegal and branded as traitors all men who assumed state office by authority of the alleged people's constitution. They were to be punished by life imprisonment at hard labor.

When the State Supreme Court invalidated the people's constitution as illegal, King asked President Tyler for federal troops to put down the Dorrite rebellion as treason. Dorr appealed to Tyler for troops to arrest King as a traitor.

The Whig President replied to King in a cautious letter expressing hope that the controversy could be settled locally. If the Dorrites resorted to open insurrection, however, he promised that the Federal Government would intervene on behalf of the old charter regime. He cited as his authority Article IV, Section 4, of the federal Constitution:

> The United States shall guarantee to every State in this Union a republican form of government, and shall protect each of them against invasion; and on application of the Legislature, or of the Executive . . . against domestic violence.

In May 1842 the King legislature proclaimed the Dorrites to be in a state of insurrection. Martial law was imposed and the state militia called out. In desperation, Dorr led his insurgents in a raid on the state arsenal at Providence to arm his followers. As the militia raced to beat them off, President Tyler alerted federal troops to stand by.

But the Dorrites were easily driven off by the artillery of the state militia. The rebellion collapsed, and Dorr fled to Connecticut. The King forces took revenge against his supporters, charging two in the legislature with treason and throwing dozens of others into jail without trial.

Hoping to rally his forces, Dorr stole back into Providence and ordered a faithful handful to dig trenches to stand off a militia attack. When the news reached King, he rushed three thousand militia to Providence. But they found only a few empty trenches; the Dorrites had melted away. So the militia arrested and jailed three hundred Providence citizens instead.

By April, 1843, however, Dorr's fight began to bear fruit even during his exile in Connecticut. The Rhode Island legislature finally adopted a new constitution with liberalized voting provisions.

Dorr made the mistake of thinking it was now safe for him to return. He was promptly arrested and on June 25, 1844, tried for treason to the state under the Algerine Act. Making certain that the jury was stacked against the defendant, Governor King also ensured the verdict by refusing to let Dorr subpoena defense witnesses because he now had no money to pay for the subpoenas. The jury sentenced him to life imprisonment.

The verdict infuriated Rhode Island's Democrats, who organized liberation societies to free Dorr. Their pressure was so successful that he was pardoned and freed a year later.

The Democrats struck back by challenging the legality of the King legislature's declaration of martial law in the crisis, as well as President Tyler's intervention on King's side. But in the Supreme Court decision of 1849, *Luther v. Borden,* the Court upheld the power of both the state legislature and the President to decide, in case of armed conflict within a state, which of two factions was the lawful government.

Dorr had one bittersweet taste of victory before ailments contracted in his foul prison dungeon caused his early death at age forty-nine. The legislature now numbered many Dorrites, elected as a result of his fight for democratic suffrage. On his deathbed, Thomas Wilson Dorr was brought word that the legislature had voted to annul the jury's verdict that had branded him guilty of treason.

Important questions of federal treason were raised again when President James Polk, infuriated by Mexico's refusal to sell the territory of New Mexico, determined to annex it forcibly. Sending American troops into the disputed area between the Nueces and Rio Grande rivers, Polk provoked a military skirmish that he used as a pretext for calling for war against Mexico for "shedding American blood on American soil."

On May 13, 1846, Congress voted Polk his war. Americans opposed to it continued to speak out vehemently. Whig congressman Abraham Lincoln branded the war as "unnecessarily and unconstitutionally begun by the President," to pursue "that rainbow" of military glory "that rises in showers of blood." He accused Polk of lying in claiming that the skirmish with Mexican troops had occurred on American soil.

Lincoln's home-town newspaper denounced him as "the Benedict Arnold of our District," and the Whigs refused to support him for renomination to the House. Another future President, Congressman Andrew Johnson, of Tennessee, accused Lincoln and other congressional opponents of the war of lacking the courage of their convictions.

If they condemned the war as wrong, Johnson challenged,

why had they voted the men and money to prosecute it? He charged them with disloyalty for encouraging the Mexicans to believe that if they continued to resist, a peace party would come to power in Washington and end the war.

But the antiwar radicals persisted in their attacks on the invasion of Mexico. Horace Greeley, powerful editor of the New York *Tribune,* called General Zachary Taylor's battles "border ruffian aggressions . . . acts of a drama of naked villainy" intended to strengthen "the Slave Power."

Angry abolitionist William Lloyd Garrison, editor of the biting weekly *Liberator,* accused Governor Briggs, of Massachusetts, of "treacherous" conduct in summoning citizens to arms for a war by a slave power against slave-free Mexico. He publicly prayed for the defeat of his own country:

> May Mexico be victorious in every conflict, until not an invading foot treads upon her soil. . . . This is for Mexico strictly a war in self-defense . . . she deserves to be crowned with success, and the United States to be covered with defeat, as a matter of justice, and for the preservation of liberty.

Polk glumly recognized the unpopularity of the Mexican War not only in New England and the North but also in some regions of the South. He dared lift no finger to punish Lincoln, Greeley, Garrison, Sumner, Parker, Emerson, and other respected Americans for treason to the war effort.

One famous New Englander, Henry David Thoreau, invented a new way to publicize antiwar sentiment and sabotage the war effort—civil disobedience. He went to jail rather than pay his Massachusetts poll tax, in order not to contribute a penny toward the war. Thoreau wrote:

> I have heard some of my townsmen say, "I should like to have them order me . . . to march to Mexico—see if I

would go"; and yet these very men have each . . . by their money, furnished a substitute. The soldier is applauded who refuses to serve in an unjust war by those who do not refuse to sustain the unjust government which makes the war.

Even though Polk's strongest support for the war was in the South, two Georgia congressmen denounced it, and South Carolina's John Calhoun demanded that all American troops be brought back to the Rio Grande. Protesting "the attainment of mere military glory," he blamed the war for damaging American prestige and violating our traditional concepts of liberty.

It was obviously impossible to sentence to death for treason hundreds of thousands, perhaps millions, of good citizens for speaking or acting against a war they considered unjust. The British Parliament, watching the acrimonious quarrel across the Atlantic, prudently decided to make their own treason laws more flexible. In 1848 the British made it more difficult to put anyone to death for idealistic opposition to his country's acts. A lower category of crime called "treason felony" was decreed, punishable by as little as five years and as much as life imprisonment. High treason was now the charge reserved for citizens accused of treachery for base motives.

The United States lacks any law distinguishing treason felony from high treason. For this reason there have been very few prosecutions under Article III, Section 3, of the Constitution. Most alleged traitors are generally prosecuted under other statutes, usually violations of laws of Congress which carry limited penalties and which juries are therefore more willing to enforce.

Americans have been reluctant to condemn legally as traitors fellow citizens whose ideas about what is patriotic differ from those of any administration in office. The requirements of patriotism often change from one administration to another. In 1856, a writer named Samuel G. Goodrich reminded Americans that not too long before, those who believed in democracy were suspect:

> We who are now familiar with democracy can hardly comprehend the odium attached to it . . . in the minds of the sober people in our neighborhood. They not only regarded it as hostile to good government, but as associated with infidelity in religion, radicalism in government and licentiousness in society. It was considered a sort of monster, born of Tom Paine, the French Revolution, foreign renegades and the Great Father of Evil, Mr. Jefferson.

Ironically, when the fashion in patriotism had changed with the War of 1812, the very Federalists who had accused Mr. Jefferson of treason were themselves accused of the same thing.

6

CIVIL WAR TREASON

A new question of treason arose in the decade of the 1850s. Were the Utah Mormons traitors for fighting a small war against the United States out of religious principle?

Because of the unpopular practice of polygamy, the Church of Jesus Christ of Latter-Day Saints had been persecuted in the East and Midwest. Its leader, Joseph Smith, had been brutally murdered. His successor, Brigham Young, led the Mormons west in 1847 to the valley of the Great Salt Lake, the Mexican territory later to become Utah. Here, at the settlement they called Deseret, they felt free to follow their religious practices outside the jurisdiction of the United States.

The end of the Mexican War, however, had put the territory under the American flag. Eastern wagon trains were soon clattering through Salt Lake City on their way to newly discovered goldfields. The Mormons found themselves once more harassed by American authority. In self-protection they applied for statehood. But at congressional hearings anti-Mormon Christian sects opposed their admission to the Union, charging them with treason, polygamy, and ritual human sacrifices.

The Mormons were accused of forcing fifteen hundred would-be immigrants to Salt Lake City to take this oath:

> You do solemnly swear, in the presence of Almighty God, his holy angels, and these witnesses, that you will avenge the blood of Joseph Smith upon this nation, and so teach your children; and that you will from this day henceforth and forever begin and carry out hostility against this nation, and keep the same a profound secret now and ever. So help you God!

Denied statehood by an indignant Congress, Utah was made a territory instead. President Millard Fillmore appointed Brigham Young as governor. Non-Mormon federal officials began arriving in Utah. Many were alcoholic hack lawyers appointed to the Utah judiciary under the spoils system, and most were hostile to the Mormons. Relations between the federal appointees and the Mormons grew bitter rapidly.

In September, 1851, Utah Associate Justice Perry C. Brocchus addressed a Mormon congregation and upbraided the Mormons for their dubious loyalty to the Government. Scolding Mormon women for accepting polygamy, he advised those in his audience to "become virtuous" instead. An uproar silenced the tirade.

Calming his furious followers, Brigham Young faced Brocchus and told him wrathfully, "Sir, if I had but crooked my finger, these good people would have torn you limb from limb—and our women would have been foremost among them!"

The Mormons were hard workers who made the desert bloom with irrigation canals and ditches, used water for the public benefit, forbade speculation in land, dealt fairly with the Indians and were respected by them, lived harmonious family lives based on the plural-wife system, and were in their own way as pious a people as any other religious sect.

Feeling persecuted by federal authority and American bigotry, however, they resisted cooperation with Washington. One Mormon band of desperadoes known as the Wolf-hunters joined Indian raiders in attacks on immigrant wagon trains en route to California. In the eyes of their fellow Americans, the real crime of the Mormons was their refusal to limit themselves to one wife apiece like other Americans.

In the elections of 1856 both Democratic and Republican candidates thundered against Mormon polygamy as a popular campaign issue translatable into votes. This agitation convinced the Mormons that a military campaign was being prepared to destroy their church. Fuel was poured on the fire when 120 immigrants in a wagon train rolled through Mormon territory abusing the Latter-Day Saints, poisoning their wells, and burning their fences. Pioneer leaders threatened to return from California with reinforcements to wipe out the Mormons.

On September 7, 1857, at Mountain Meadows in southwest Utah, a wagon train was attacked by an Indian band accompanied by Mormon Wolf-hunters. A three-day siege brought casualties to both sides. A truce was arranged when Mormon militia under John Doyle Lee appeared with a white flag. The immigrants accepted Lee's offer to escort them to safety.

But the entire company, with the exception of some children, was then brutally massacred. An outraged President Buchanan told Congress that Young and his followers apparently were determined "to come into collision with the Government of the United States." Young was removed as Utah's governor, and Buchanan ordered fifteen hundred troops, under Colonel Albert Sidney Johnson, into the territory.

Young defied the President. Declaring martial law, he ordered all Mormons to arms to keep federal troops off Utah soil. Mormon cavalry burned three wagon trains of federal supplies and captured eight hundred oxen from a fourth. Johnson captured Lee and executed him for the Mountain Meadows massacre. But the onset of winter forced both sides into bivouac until spring.

By then Buchanan had managed to reach an accommodation with the Mormons through their spokesman in Washington. He was anxious to extricate himself from the uncertain expedition to Utah that political foes were mocking as "Buchanan's blunder." The Mormons were induced to save face for the President by making a formal acknowledgment of Washington's authority in Utah and allowing federal troops to remain for a while as long as they did not attack any Mormons.

In the summer of 1858 a peace commission from Washington brought the Mormons a Presidential pardon for their treason. Brigham Young went to prison several times before he died in 1877, survived by twenty-five wives and fifty-six children, but never once for treason. His crime was a stubborn refusal to pay alimony to his nineteenth wife after she had divorced him.

Treason of another sort by fanatical abolitionists was also a Government headache. Kansas sheepman John Brown conceived the idea of carving an independent republic of fugitive slaves out of the southern Appalachians to serve as a refuge and fortress for blacks escaping from the South.

He drew up a constitution for the proposed republic and was chosen by eleven white and thirty-five black followers as its commander in chief. To get the arms the new republic would need, Brown led eighteen followers, four of them black, in a guerrilla raid on the federal arsenal at Harper's Ferry, Virginia. On the night of October 16, 1859, they seized the arsenal, killed the mayor, and took sixty leading citizens as hostages.

Calling out the Virginia militia, Governor Henry Wise frantically wired President Buchanan for federal troops. John Brown urged slaves in the town to join his ranks, but none dared fire a gun beside him. They remembered too well the hundred blacks who had been shot and the twenty who had been hung when Nat Turner and only six fellow slaves had run amok in Virginia twenty-eight years earlier.

Before dawn one of Brown's sons was dead and another wounded. When Colonel Robert E. Lee arrived with a company of marines from Washington and forced Brown's surrender, they found only Brown and six other survivors in the locomotive-roundhouse to which the raiders were forced to retreat.

Panic spread through a South frightened of a slave uprising, then quickly gave way to vengeful wrath. John Brown, wounded after his capture, was rushed to trial only eight days later. His counsel urged him to plead insanity. Many abolitionists, in fact, were convinced that his fanaticism and wild schemes indicated mental instability. But Brown refused to save his life by discrediting the soundness of his cause.

The jury found him guilty of "treason and conspiring and advising with slaves and other rebels, and murder in the first degree." Writing to his children that he was content "to die for God's eternal truth on the scaffold as in any other way," Brown was hanged on December 2, 1859.

Millions of conservative northerners defended his execution by the South, arguing that he had not been hanged as an abolitionist but as a traitor to the laws of the United States. Every American owed his loyalty to the Government, they insisted, however much he might hate some of its institutions.

But Ralph Waldo Emerson predicted that "that new saint . . . will make the gallows glorious like the cross."

"In firing his gun," cried William Lloyd Garrison, "John Brown has merely told us what time of day it is. It is high noon . . . thank God!" Garrison himself had risked arrest for treason by publicly burning copies of the Fugitive Slave Act and the Constitution, which he renounced as "a covenant with death and an agreement with hell!"

The Civil War raised questions of treason more profound than any since the founding of the Republic. Did states alienated from the Federal Government have the right to secede to form their own independent nation? Or was this a conspiracy forbidden by the Constitution, making all Americans who joined it traitors to the Union, not southern patriots?

Southerners pointed to the agitation of radical abolitionists such as Garrison, who for years had been demanding that the North secede from the Union, casting the South and slavery adrift. None of *them* had ever been punished. Why should secession be treason only when the South wanted it?

Ironically, General Robert E. Lee had insisted that every southerner's first loyalty ought to be to the Federal Government.

"I wish to live under no other government," he insisted, "and there is no sacrifice I am not ready to make for the preservation of the Union." He added, "I wish for no other flag than the Star Spangled Banner and no other air than 'Hail Columbia.' " He considered secession "nothing but revolution!"

Yet once the fat was in the fire, Lee asserted that his "loyalty to Virginia ought to take precedence over that which is due the Federal Government." Far from enthusiastic about the rebel cause he had been prevailed upon to lead, he admitted sadly to General William S. Harney, a southerner loyal to Washington, "I had no idea of taking any part in this matter. I wanted to stay at Arlington and raise potatoes for my family, but my friends forced me into it."

Plots to slay Abraham Lincoln were assessed as either high treason or southern patriotism, depending on the geography of the judgment. Lincoln protested the close escort of Pinkerton police assigned to him as President-elect, forcing Allen Pinkerton to reveal that there were several serious conspiracies afoot to kill him. Lincoln was astonished.

"Why would anyone want to do that?"

"Mr. President," Pinkerton sighed, "you simply cannot comprehend the mad, hysterical feeling prevailing against you in and around Baltimore."

But Lincoln could not take seriously the threats on his life. That was why he was insufficiently protected at Ford's Theater the night John Wilkes Booth made history. Lincoln appreciated the wrath of southerners frustrated by northern policy against slavery but could not bring himself to believe that they would assassinate him for it.

On July 17, 1862, an act of Congress prescribed a ten-thousand-dollar fine and punishment of from five years at hard labor to execution for anyone convicted of insurrection, conspiracy, or treason against the government. Now every American who aided the Confederacy by either word or deed was put on notice that he could pay for his political sympathies with his life.

7

"A SCURVY LOT THEY ARE"

Southern spies scorned northern treason laws. Rose Greenhow, an attractive, socially prominent Washington widow, declared, "Instead of loving and worshipping the old flag of the Stars and Stripes, I see in it only the symbol of abolition—of murder, plunder, oppression, and shame."

Learning of a federal plan to attack the Confederate Army at Manassas, she rushed a secret warning to General Pierre Beauregard. His subsequent victory led Confederate President Jefferson Davis to acknowledge the South's debt to her. She charmed military secrets out of vulnerable Union satraps until caught by Allen Pinkerton and jailed. Her influence in Washington society was so great that plans to try her as a spy were dropped, and she was released in a prisoner exchange.

Another celebrated female traitor was Belle Boyd, a beautiful young Virginian girl. At seventeen she shot and killed a Union sergeant for trying to force his way into the Boyd home. Gallant federal officers, smitten by her crinoline charms, decided that Belle's offense had been "justifiable homicide."

A passionate Confederate, she carried secret intelligence through Union lines dozens of times. The quartering of northern officers in the Boyd home under martial law provided her with vital information for the Confederate Army. Once she braved heavy fire from both sides to cross a battlefield with a warning for Stonewall Jackson that enabled him to save his forces from a Union trap.

"I thank you for myself and for the army," Jackson wrote her, "for the immense service that you have rendered your country day."

When Belle sent Jackson a new warning via a Rebel soldier who was actually a Union secret agent, it fell into the hands of Secretary of War Edwin M. Stanton. Jailed, she was freed in a prisoner exchange with Richmond, where she was welcomed by a band and where Confederate troops presented arms in her honor.

The Conscription Act of March 1, 1863, made it an act of disloyalty to refuse to be drafted for the Union Army—unless you could afford to pay three hundred dollars for a substitute. Many workers considered the bill discriminatory against the poor. American laborers especially resented being drafted for what they saw as freeing the black man to compete with them. Draft officials were driven off the Pennsylvania coalfields by the tough Molly Maguires.

The first draft lottery in New York touched off wild rioting and violence. A mob of thousands broke into an arsenal, passed out carbines, and surged through the streets, burning buildings and smashing draft offices. They cut down telephone poles, tore up tracks, and overturned horse-cars. Bodies of lynched Negroes swung from lampposts all along Clarkson Street, flaming human torches in the night.

Thirteen regiments of federal troops had to be taken out of the war from General George Meade's army at Gettysburg. Rushed to New York on express trains over cleared tracks, they arrived just in time to prevent the burning of the *Tribune* building. Mobs sought to lynch editor Horace Greeley, blaming him for championing the cause of emancipation.

Throwing up breastworks along Ninth Avenue, the rioters fought the Army until their ammunition was exhausted. When Meade's troops finally restored order, over fifteen hundred rioters and troops lay dead—a greater loss of life than any caused by the most celebrated battles of the Civil War.

Lincoln was forced to take other fighting units away from Meade to prevent similar explosions in other cities. Meade had to put off pursuing Lee and the badly battered Confederate Army as they retreated from Gettysburg, possibly robbing the North of a quick victory.

The draft rioters of New York had unquestionably violated the treason statute of the Constitution—"levying war against" the United States and "giving aid and comfort" to their enemies. They were also in violation of Lincoln's own Treason Act of 1862. But no charges of treason were brought.

Lincoln also had his hands full with citizens known as Copperheads—northerners with southern sympathies. Because they were so numerous and some held high office, Congress set up a committee to investigate the loyalty of all federal employees. It soon became known as "the office of secret accusations." Government clerks, terrified of losing their jobs, agreed to spy on fellow employees and department heads, reporting all "suspicious" talk or contacts.

In September, 1862, Lincoln issued a proclamation suspending the writ of habeas corpus that allows lawyers to free illegally detained defendants under the Sixth Amendment. Lincoln wanted the power to keep Copperheads and draft opponents in jail to restrain their damage to the war effort. The alternative was clogging the courts with difficult-to-prove treason trials.

Lincoln was promptly attacked as a military despot who was violating the Bill of Rights out of expediency. Public indignation mounted when loyal northerners were mistakenly arrested and jailed along with draft resisters, Copperheads, and spies. The War Department was forced to free all those arrested under Lincoln's decree who agreed to take a loyalty oath.

Perhaps the most important Copperhead was Ohio's Clement L. Vallandigham, congressman, lawyer, and newspaper editor who had opposed the Civil War bitterly from the start. He even entered secret negotiations with the French to get Napoleon III to force peace talks upon the North.

In 1863, General A. E. Burnside angrily issued a general order stating, "The habit of declaring sympathy for the enemy will not be allowed" in his military district. Violators, he warned, would be arrested for treason and executed. Vallandigham defied him.

Continuing to denounce Lincoln, the Union, and the war, the Copperhead leader called upon midwesterners to ignore Burnside's order. Arrested, he was court-martialed and sentenced by Burnside to imprisonment in Fort Warren for the duration of the war. But Lincoln changed the sentence to a more appropriate and humane one—"deportation to Confederate territory." Vallandigham approved his banishment, announcing scornfully, "I do not *wish* to belong to the United States!"

His defiance inspired Edward Everett Hale to write the famous novel *The Man without a Country*. Appearing in the *Atlantic* for December, 1863, it inspired a surge of patriotic feeling throughout the North. Vallandigham, however, was convinced that the tide of public sentiment was turning against Lincoln, the Republicans, and the war. He assured Confederate President Jefferson Davis that the Democrats stood a good chance of winning the 1864 elections on an antiwar platform.

Making his way to Canada, Vallandigham sought to help

organize the opposition to the Republicans from there. New York's Governor Seymour echoed his charges that the real treason to America was the Administration's destruction of free institutions in the North to put down rebellion in the South. At public meetings Seymour and other Copperheads denounced arbitrary arrests, Lincoln's suspension of the Sixth Amendment, and Vallandigham's deportation. The Democratic State Convention of Ohio defiantly nominated Vallandigham for governor.

Lincoln defended his policies by pointing out that if such outspoken "traitors to the Union" as Lee and Breckinridge had been arrested for treason before the war, "the insurgent cause would be much weaker." He predicted, "I shall be blamed for having made too few arrests, rather than too many." And he asked, "Must I shoot a simple-minded soldier-boy, who deserts, while I must not touch a hair of a wily agitator who induces him to desert? . . . To silence the agitator and save the boy is not only constitutional, but withal a great mercy."

He did not order Vallandigham's arrest, however, when the latter returned to Ohio in 1864 to wage an unsuccessful campaign for governor. The Copperhead vowed that he was not trying to aid the Confederacy, simply to restore "the Union as it was." He appealed his arrest and military trial as a civilian by Burnside, but the Supreme Court refused to hear the case in order not to undermine military authority.

Two years later, however, in a decision called *Ex parte Milligan,* the Court ruled on the issue in the case of Lambdin P. Milligan. Arrested in 1864 and charged with "conspiracy, affording aid and comfort to rebels and inciting insurrection," Milligan and three Indiana Copperheads had been found guilty of treason and sentenced to hang by a military commission.

Lincoln had put off signing the order for execution, but President Andrew Johnson had signed it after Lincoln's assassination. Milligan's lawyer appealed to the Supreme Court on grounds that he had been unlawfully tried by a military tribunal while civilian courts were available and open. By a vote of 5 to 4, the Supreme Court agreed, finding that neither the President nor Congress had power to suspend the constitutional safeguards of citizens during time of war.

When the Civil War was over and the dead counted, the awkward question rose of who should then be arrested for treason. The vengeful cry, "Hang Jefferson Davis!" rang through the North. President Johnson promised, "I'm going to hang that traitor to a tree!"

The sacrificial scapegoat was captured by Union soldiers in Georgia on May 10, 1865. Jailed at Fort Monroe, he was kept in leg irons by Major General Nelson A. Miles for four days. Guarded day and night, he was proudly exhibited by Miles to visitors like a rare captive tiger. The Government indicted him for treason, but two years went by without a trial.

Johnson knew that there was no evidence linking Davis to Lincoln's assassination. Whether the southern rebellion could be made to stick as a treason charge in court was a moot question which, incidentally, was never settled judicially.

Horace Greeley was indignant at the injustice of keeping Davis under lock and key so long without his day in court. He forced the Government to set a bail bond of $100,000 under the prisoner's right to a "speedy and public trial by an impartial jury" (Sixth Amendment). The money was raised from a group of prominent Americans, and the ex-President of the Confederacy was set free in May, 1867.

A storm of angry northern criticism blasted Greeley for his act of humanity. He replied defiantly, "So long as any man was seeking to overthrow our government he was my enemy; from the hour in which he laid down his arms, he was my formerly erring countryman." In the South, of course, Jefferson Davis continued to be revered as a great patriot; only those who had refused to support the Rebel cause were regarded as traitors.

The bitterness of the treason question did not die easily after the war. In 1865, Missouri, where Copperhead sentiment had been strong, passed an amendment to the state constitution requiring citizens wishing to teach, preach, or vote to swear that they had been loyal to the Union. Congress compelled all attorneys practicing in federal courts to take a similar oath vowing past loyalty.

Two years later, in the cases of *Cummings v. Missouri* and *Ex parte Garland,* the Supreme Court ruled both requirements unconstitutional in a 5 to 4 decision. Nevertheless, almost a century later, similar federal and state loyalty-oath requirements were again demanded to determine political purity.

In 1872, the Republican party under President Ulysses S. Grant was badly split. Its liberal wing attacked the Administration for seeking to grab Santo Domingo. Feeling they could not support Grant for renomination, the radical Republicans broke away and ran their own candidates. They were denounced as traitors by party regulars, who reminded them of Decatur's famous toast: "My country, right or wrong!"

Carl Schurz replied, "Our country, right or wrong! When right, to be kept right; when wrong, to be put right!"

The debate over those two points of view was still as hot as ever almost a century later when superpatriot groups, angered by opposition to the Vietnam war, used Decatur-inspired car stickers reading: "America—Love It or Leave It!" Dissenters replied with their version of Schurz's sentiment: "America—Love It and Change It!"

Schurz, along with celebrated Americans such as William Jennings Bryan, Mark Twain, Samuel Gompers, and Harvard president Charles Eliot, formed the Anti-Imperialist League in

1898 to oppose the Spanish-American War. Jingoists defended the war on grounds that it was obviously America's Manifest Destiny to civilize countries that "practised barbarism."

The Anti-Imperialist League observed caustically that when "civilizers" stooped to barbarism to end barbarism, it was hard to tell the barbarians apart. "Imperialism is hostile to liberty and tends toward militarism," the league declared, "an evil from which it is our glory to be free."

No treason charges were brought against the war dissenters, who were simply swept aside as cranks and crackpots.

After only ten weeks of fighting, Cuba and the Philippines were in American hands, while the Anti-Imperialist League pondered the futility of their dissent.

Violent clashes between labor and capital around the turn of the century introduced new concepts of treason. The radicalization of the labor movement, with the rise of Socialists, anarchists, and Wobblies (Industrial Workers of the World, I.W.W.), frightened the big corporations. The newspapers they controlled began attacking labor militants as dangerous traitors plotting revolution.

When three men were jailed for bombings in labor battles in the western minefields, President Theodore Roosevelt declared that, guilty or not, they were "undesirable citizens." Thousands of angry labor sympathizers began wearing buttons inscribed: "I Am an Undesirable Citizen."

Jack London gave his version of treason: "A strikebreaker is a traitor to his God, his country, his wife, his family and his class."

Muckraking journalists branded as traitors the robber barons who perverted the Government for their own ends, along with the elected and appointed officials who served them as hirelings. In 1906 David Graham Phillips wrote a stinging exposé for *Cosmopolitan,* called "The Treason of the Senate." He accused

Rhode Island's Senator Nelson W. Aldrich of leading a conspiracy to betray the American public, manipulating legislation to enrich powerful special interests.

"A scurvy lot they are . . . with their smirking and cringing and voluble palaver about God and patriotism," Phillips wrote angrily. They were, he said, traitors not only to all the people but also to the political parties that had elected them to the Senate.

Although no tycoons were indicted for treason, Roosevelt assumed the mantle of a social reformer. Calling himself a "trust-buster," he began introducing bills to put mild curbs on the more outrageous buccaneering of the big corporations. But the trusts continued to prosper by controlling legislation through big political contributions.

"That's the system," Lincoln Steffens, most famous of the muckrakers, explained in 1920. "It's an organization of social treason, and the political boss is the chief traitor. . . . They buy the people's leaders."

The big corporations waited for an opportunity to counterattack those they considered traitors to the American free enterprise system—muckrakers, Socialists, anarchists, and labor radicals. Their chance came with the outbreak of World War I. Public wrath was aroused against pacifists and the political Left, who were lumped with German spies and sympathizers as dangerous traitors.

The most celebrated case was the arrest and trial of radical labor leaders Tom Mooney and Warren Billings. They were charged with exploding a bomb on a crowded street-corner during a Preparedness Day parade on San Francisco's Market Street on July 22, 1916. Ten persons were killed, forty others maimed. The defendants were prosecuted by District Attorney Charles M. Fickert, who knew that the San Francisco Chamber of Commerce was anxious to discredit strike organizers. A conviction could win its support of his nomination for governor.

Tom Mooney's friendship with anarchist Alexander Berkman, Fickert charged, indicated his terroristic and antimilitaristic motives in bombing the parade. William Randolph Hearst's *Examiner* demanded the arrest of all known or suspected radicals in California. The press carried distorted and fabricated stories, planted by the city's Bomb Bureau and by Fickert, to incriminate Mooney and Billings and prejudice any jury against them.

At the trials the chief prosecution witnesses were obvious perjurers and people with shady pasts. Almost all contradicted themselves, and each other, under cross-examination. Several later recanted their testimony, admitting they had been told what to say. With no reliable evidence to offer, Fickert sought to win a conviction by waving the flag.

"This American flag was what they desired to offend," he cried. "They offended that by killing the women and men that worshipped it. Here is another photograph of Mrs. Van Loo dying on the streets of our city, and in a feeble hand she holds the American flag, and if that flag is to continue to wave, you must put an end to such acts as these!"

He demanded the death penalty. "Gentlemen, the very life of the nation is at stake. No foreign foes were on our land at this time; some traitor, some murderous villain, with his associates, perpetrated this crime. . . . The crime was against the flag; the crime was against the Constitution of the United States; the crime was against the laws of this government."

The defendants were tried separately. The jury brought in a verdict against Billings of murder in the first degree, recommending life imprisonment. When Mooney was brought to trial in January, 1917, the United States was on the verge of war. Peace sentiment was already suspect as treason.

Prosecutor Edward A. Cuhna, Fickert's chief assistant, accused Mooney of being part of an anarchist conspiracy to weaken America by sabotaging "Preparedness"—the catchword signifying national defense. Proof against Mooney rested largely on the eyewitness testimony of Frank C. Oxman, alleged to be a wealthy Oregon cattleman.

"Oxman was by far the most important of these witnesses," Judge Franklin A. Griffin later declared. "There is no question but that he made a profound impression on the jury. . . . He is the pivot around which all of the other evidence in the case revolves." When the jury found Mooney guilty of murder in the first degree, Griffin ordered him to hang.

But attorneys of the two convicted men were convinced that there had been a terrible miscarriage of justice. There was good reason to believe that the bombs had actually been the work of either German agents or Mexican revolutionaries, but neither lead had been diligently pursued. Evidence was found that Mooney could not have been anywhere near the bomb when it was thrown: a photo showing him with other spectators watching the parade from a rooftop a mile from the explosion. A jeweler's street clock established the time.

Fickert's office had suppressed this photo. Witnesses who had come forward to prove Mooney's innocence had been gotten rid of. Then it was found that Oxman had committed perjury at a previous trial. Evidence grew that his testimony against Mooney had also been false and that Fickert knew it.

Fremont Older, editor of the San Francisco *Bulletin,* tried to reveal these facts, but the paper's publishers refused to let him. He quit and became editor of the rival *Morning Call* in order to expose the legal conspiracy against the convicted radicals. A nationwide uproar led to demands for Fickert's ouster.

"The people leading this fight against me are the anarchists," Fickert accused. "Their main reason for wanting me out of office is that they fear prosecution. There were more than a hundred people concerned in the Preparedness Day bomb plot, and it is this anarchist element . . . that seeks my recall."

Growing wartime hysteria over radicalism and disloyalty

helped smother the facts. Theodore Roosevelt rushed to Fickert's defense with a published telegram calling the issue one between patriotism and anarchy: "ALL WHO DIRECTLY OR INDIRECTLY ASSAIL YOU FOR ANY REASON SHOULD BE PROMPTLY DEPRIVED OF THEIR CITIZENSHIP." Roosevelt was soon attacking all radical labor and peace groups as "the Bolsheviki of America."

On the eve of a referendum to decide the recall of Fickert, a bomb exploded outside the Governor's Mansion in Sacramento. Next day the recall motion was voted down. Although no evidence linked fifty-three Sacramento members of the I.W.W. to the bombing, they were jailed and eventually prosecuted by the Federal Government for violating the wartime Sedition Act.

Fickert won his nomination for governor, campaigned promising "complete suppression of sedition on the home front," and lost. When the war ended, Mooney's execution was only a month away. Then Fremont Older's *Call* published a bombshell—transcripts of conversations taken from Fickert's "bugged" telephone. They proved all the charges made against him by Mooney-Billings sympathizers. In a wild fury Fickert confronted Older in San Francisco's Palace Hotel and assaulted him.

Governor Stephens now acted to save Mooney from the gallows, commuting his sentence to life imprisonment. Not at all grateful, Mooney wrote the governor angrily:

> It is my life you are dealing with. I demand that you revoke your commutation of my death sentence to a living death. . . . I am innocent. I demand a new and a fair trial or my unconditional liberty through a pardon. If I were guilty of the crime for which I have been unjustly convicted, hanging would be too good for me. Then why commute my sentence to life?

The Colfax *Record* had an answer:

The reason that Mooney and Billings are in prison is because a majority of the people of the State of California
want them there and the Supreme Court and the Governor
dare not disobey that majority. It is quite beside the point
whether or not they are guilty of the particular crime of
which they were charged and convicted. The question is:
Are Mooney and Billings the sort of people we want to run
at large? We have decided this in the negative and we have
locked them up.

The crusade to free Mooney and Billings grew steadily after
the war and was part of every labor and radical rally. Mounting
labor unrest, a Seattle general strike, and a labor-sponsored
Mooney Congress alarmed big-business interests.

They were convinced that a Bolshevik plot of revolution was
afoot when unknown persons mailed bombs to many prominent
symbols of the Establishment on the eve of May Day, 1919. Two
bombs went to Fickert and Cuhna, who, like the other targets,
did not open them and were unhurt. Two anarchists were arrested, but no charges were filed. One suspect was simply
deported; the other was alleged to have fallen out of a four-
teenth-story window while in custody, under unexplained circumstances.

Fickert sought to win reelection as district attorney on the
slogan, "American Flag or the Red Flag," but lost.

As new evidence kept turning up to prove the innocence of
Mooney and Billings, even seven of the jurors who had convicted
Mooney appealed to the governor to pardon them.

Mooney was offered a parole in 1927 but refused it: "I am
absolutely innocent. I will not accept anything short of Pardon."

A National Mooney-Billings Committee—sponsored by such
famous Americans as Roger Baldwin, Clarence Darrow, John
Dewey, Arthur Garfield Hays, Sinclair Lewis, Lincoln Steffens,

and Rabbi Stephen Wise—now demanded absolute pardons for both prisoners.

"Mooney can stand prison," Socialist leader Norman Thomas said, "better than we can stand having him there!"

Now a worldwide cause célèbre, the case began making new headlines in the *Manchester Guardian, The New York Times,* and other major organs of international influence. Albert Einstein, Bertrand Russell, and H. G. Wells pleaded for the prisoned martyrs. Over five hundred ministers, the Federal Council of Churches of Christ in America, the National Catholic Welfare Council, dozens of governors, mayors, and congressmen added their voices.

"If Tom Mooney is not freed," declared Theodore Dreiser, "he should, by rights, be taken out of prison by force!"

President Herbert Hoover appointed the Wickersham Committee to study the case, then suppressed its findings. In 1932, a Democratic Congress demanded that the report be made public. It revealed that the impartial Government investigation had found the two radicals to have been victims of a gross injustice. But they were still not freed.

The California State Assembly itself passed a resolution in 1937 declaring Mooney innocent and demanding a full pardon. A Gallup poll one year later showed that 66 per cent of Americans agreed. But it was not until January 7, 1939—five days after the election of Culbert L. Olson, California's first Democratic governor of the twentieth century—that Tom Mooney was declared innocent and freed from San Quentin Prison.

He was now partly deaf, in ill health, divorced, penniless, and unemployed. In October, Billings also was set free. They had spent a total of twenty-two years of their lives behind bars for a "traitorous crime against the flag and the Constitution and the laws"—a crime they had not committed but had been punished for in a climate of wartime hysteria.

8

TREASON
IN WORLD WAR I

Another labor martyr of World War I was Socialist leader Eugene V. Debs. On June 16, 1918, while addressing a labor rally in Canton, Ohio, on behalf of Mooney and Billings, Debs made no bones about his opposition to the war, even though he knew Secret Service agents were taking notes in the crowd.

"You need to know that you are fit for something better than slavery and cannon fodder," he declared. "I am opposed to every war but one. I am for that war with heart and soul, and that is the worldwide war of social revolution. In that war I am prepared to fight in any way the ruling class may make it necessary, even on the barricades!"

Arrested, he was sentenced to ten years in jail and deprived of his citizenship. "The government has made me a citizen of the world," he observed dryly. Running from prison as the Socialist candidate for President in the 1920 elections, he received almost a million votes. President Woodrow Wilson, who could not forgive Debs's refusal to support the war, would not pardon him, insisting, "This man was a traitor to his country!" It was President Warren Harding who pardoned Debs in 1921, although he did not restore his citizenship.

Ironically, while campaigning for the League of Nations after the war, Wilson admitted to a crowd in St. Louis, "Who does not know that the seed of war in the modern world is industrial and commercial rivalry? The real reason that the war . . . took place was that Germany was afraid her commercial rivals were going to get the better of her, and . . . they thought Germany would get the commercial advantage of them."

Yet Wilson had jailed Debs for saying exactly the same thing—that World War I had been an imperialistic conflict for markets, not a crusade to save the world for democracy.

On April 6, 1917, ten weeks after Congress declared war on Germany, it passed an Espionage Act. Conviction for aiding the enemy, obstructing recruiting, or sabotaging military discipline carried punishments of up to a twenty-thousand-dollar fine and twenty years in prison. The Postmaster General was authorized to exclude from the mails newspapers, periodicals, and all printed matter alleged to be treasonable or seditious.

A Socialist named Schenck was the first to be convicted on a charge of impeding recruiting by writing pamphlets condemning the war as an imperialist struggle in which workers of the world could have no interest. His case was appealed to the Supreme Court as a violation of his right to free speech. But Justice John Haynes Holmes upheld the legality of the Espionage Act on grounds that encouraging draft resistance was a "clear and present danger" to the nation in arms.

"When a nation is at war," Holmes declared, "many things that might be said in time of peace are such a hindrance to its effort that their utterance will not be endured as long as men fight, and that no court could regard them as protected by any constitutional right."

The American Civil Liberties Union, organized during World War I to protect the constitutional rights of Americans opposed to the war, sharply dissented. Holmes himself later agreed that the "clear and present danger" doctrine could not be used to choke off radical ideas, no matter how unpopular or how uncomfortable the Government found them.

Not until over a year after the Espionage Act did Congress pass an amendment called the Sedition Act. The new law was aimed specifically at Socialists and pacifists, prescribing severe penalties for interfering with the war effort; using "disloyal, profane, scurrilous or abusive language" about the American Government, Constitution, flag, or armed forces; or urging a cutback in production of war materials.

Used to imprison Debs and other Socialist leaders, the Sedition Act was first challenged when a young Russian-born immigrant named Abrams, with four co-workers in a New York hat factory, printed and distributed leaflets attacking the Government for sending an American expeditionary force against the new Red Army in Siberia. Arrested, they protested that they supported the war against Germany and considered it weakened by diverting troops to interfere with the revolutionary struggle in Russia. But they had urged workers to strike rather than produce arms for use against the Soviet Union.

Found guilty, they were sentenced to twenty years in jail. The Supreme Court upheld their conviction, but Justices Holmes and Brandeis dissented. There was no "clear and present danger" to the war effort in this case, Holmes wrote, so it amounted to a violation of the First Amendment.

"I believe the defendants had as much right to publish [their leaflets] as the Government has to publish the Constitution of the United States now vainly invoked by them," Holmes argued.

He added, "We should be eternally vigilant against attempts to check the expression of opinions that we loathe and believe to be fraught with death, unless . . . an immediate check is required to save the country." In 1921, President Harding commuted the defendants' sentences, but they were deported to Russia.

For several years before America went to war with Germany in April, 1917, millions of Americans of German and Irish extraction had bitterly opposed any aid to Great Britain. Wilson, who at first tried to keep the United States neutral, nevertheless detested them as "hyphenated Americans."

Leader of the anti-British movement was a well-to-do Irish-American lawyer, Jeremiah O'Leary, who had been president of the American Truth Society. He offered Wilson the society's support in the 1916 Presidential elections if Wilson stuck to his neutrality policy. Wilson wired him contemptuously: "I WOULD FEEL DEEPLY MORTIFIED TO HAVE YOU OR ANYBODY LIKE YOU VOTE FOR ME. SINCE YOU HAVE ACCESS TO MANY DISLOYAL AMERICANS AND I HAVE NOT I WILL ASK YOU TO CONVEY THIS MESSAGE TO THEM."

Soon after America entered the war, O'Leary organized an American branch of the anti-British Sinn Fein society. He was indicted for "conspiracy to commit treason" in violation of the Espionage Act. Britain was now America's war ally; thus anti-British agitation was now disloyal.

At the trial the Government proved that O'Leary's propaganda had been financed from Germany but could not prove that he knew it. A defendant indicted with him, Madame de Victorica, turned state's witness, but her testimony was discredited when O'Leary proved that she was an admitted spy and dope addict. Another witness was exposed as a perjurer. Deciding that the case had not been proved, the jury freed O'Leary.

These were dangerous times for dissent. Superpatriotic mobs frequently took the law into their own hands. Any public criticism of the war or of war profiteers often brought the cry of "Traitor!" Six victims were painted yellow; many were hung until almost dead (three were cut down too late); sixty-four were tarred and feathered; fifty-five kidnapped and whipped; eleven hundred were forcibly driven out of the country.

Government punishment was no less severe. A St. Louis woman went to jail for ten years for writing in a letter to a newspaper, "I am for the people and the Government is for the profiteers." There were sentences of fifteen years for talking against the draft; ten years for opposing the Liberty Loans; twenty years for calling the Government a liar, for approving the sinking of the *Lusitania,* and for predicting a German victory.

Sabotage of the war effort by corporation executives received gentler treatment. In order to conserve steel for guns, tanks, locomotives, and ships needed for the war, the War Industries Board ordered Detroit's industrial leaders to cut back the production of cars. They refused, informing board head Bernard M. Baruch that they would use all the steel and coal they wanted for cars, and he couldn't stop them, war or no war. They gave in only when he threatened to seize all their coal and shut down their plants.

Baruch also clashed with the steel industry, which was gouging the Government on defense orders. Baruch deplored the fact that profits were immense. But the steel barons would not stop war profiteering until President Wilson, at Baruch's appeal, warned that the Government would take over steel production.

The labor unions, forbidden to strike for the duration of the war, protested the disinclination of the Justice Department to prosecute striking industrialists for sedition.

Western nations were seriously worried by the emergence of the Russian Revolution during the war. In 1919, Britain, France, and the United States mounted a joint, unsuccessful expedition to Siberia to overthrow the new Soviet regime. Leaders of the U.S.S.R. grew convinced that the West would not allow a Communist government to survive as a threat to world capitalism.

So they developed the Comintern, a Communist international organization. Its representatives organized Communist parties directed from Moscow. The Kremlin planned to use them as centers of subversion and espionage against nations hostile to the Soviet Union.

In January, 1919, Ludwig C. A. K. Martens, a member of the Russian Communist party, was sent by the Comintern to help organize the Workers' (later the Communist) party in the United States. Members recruited from the radical labor movement were encouraged to feel that anything they could do to help the Soviet Union, the new "workers' paradise," automatically helped the cause of the working class everywhere.

Attorney General A. Mitchell Palmer took the view that *all* "radically inclined individuals," not only Communists, were dangerous to the security of the United States. In August, 1919, he created a General Investigation Division (later the F.B.I.) of the Department of Justice. J. Edgar Hoover, a young operative who headed it as Palmer's special assistant, was ordered to compile a list of sixty thousand "suspected radicals."

On the night of January 1, 1920, Palmer-ordered raids in thirty-three cities seized over four thousand political and labor militants in mass arrests. Labor saw the raids as an attempt to intimidate its organizers from calling strikes because of low wages, high prices, and unemployment. After being jailed for up to a week, almost all the "radically inclined individuals" arrested had to be released for lack of any valid evidence against them.

Felix Frankfurter, who had been chairman of the War Labor Policies Board, joined a dozen prominent lawyers in condemning the Palmer raids as illegal. Palmer called the lawyers "Communists," and Frankfurter's name was added to the G.I.D.'s list of suspected subversives. By the time the raids stopped in May, the list had grown to 450,000.

Yet in his own book, *Masters of Deceit,* J. Edgar Hoover noted that Communist-party membership was still under 12,400 even two years later. And Communist candidates in the presidential elections eight years later still could not attract even fifty thousand votes. Referring to the Palmer raids, a later President, Harry S Truman, called them "a terrible thing . . . the 'Communist hysteria' program of its day."

The raids probably radicalized many workers who until then had regarded their grievances as directed only against big business, not against the Government. When citizens are oppressed by a majority, Lord Acton warned in 1877, "there is no appeal, no redemption, no refuge but treason."

During the 1920s American industrialists, worried about the spread of the Communist movement, watched with deep interest the steps taken by their counterparts in Europe to develop an anti-Communist force. First in Italy, then in Germany, big business interests financed a militaristic movement called fascism. Led by Mussolini in Italy and Hitler in Germany, Fascist storm troops terrorized all opposition in order to seize power in the democracies and establish a dictatorship.

On November 25, 1922, Benito Mussolini led his Blackshirts in a march on Rome, overthrew the Government, and declared himself dictator. Two weeks later the Scripps-Howard press featured an interview with the newly elected commander of the American Legion, Alvin Owsley, who declared that the Legion likewise stood ready to take over the American Government if necessary. He warned that the world spread of revolutionary doctrine had to be taken seriously, and the Legion was fighting every element threatening democracy.

"Should the day ever come," he declared, "when they menace

the freedom of our representative government, the Legion would not hesitate to take things into its own hands—to fight the Reds as the Fascisti of Italy fought them."

Edward A. Rumely served as an American link to the Nazi (National-Socialist) forces in Germany, who, under Adolf Hitler, sought to emulate Mussolini's coup d'etat in Italy. Rumely had been arrested in July, 1918, on charges of perjury, for concealing the fact that he had been an agent of Imperial Germany in buying and publishing the New York *Evening Mail* with German funds. A famous American, Henry Ford, had rushed to Washington to try to save him from indictment, but Rumely was sentenced to a year and a day in the Atlanta Penitentiary.

"Edward A. Rumely was for years the secret paid agent of the German Government," declared George Harvey, American ambassador to England. "Rumely's close, if not closest, friend during the past six years has been Henry Ford."

Ford's sympathies with Germany persisted in his postwar support of Hitler's anti-Semitic Nazi movement. When Ford was being boomed as a Presidential candidate in 1923, the Chicago *Tribune* quoted Hitler's tribute: "We look to Heinrich Ford as the leader of the growing Fascist movement in America."

At the 1923 trial of Hitler for his unsuccessful Munich beer-hall putsch, Herr Auer, vice president of the Bavarian Diet, testified: "The Bavarian Diet has long had the information that the Hitler movement was partly financed by an American anti-Semitic chief, who is Henry Ford. . . . Herr Hitler openly boasts of Mr. Ford's support. . . . A photograph of Mr. Ford hangs in Herr Hitler's quarters." The charge was frequently reported in the *Manchester Guardian, Berliner Tageblatt,* and *The New York Times.*

It was never denied. In a book he wrote in 1938, *I Knew Hitler,* Nazi agent Kurt K. W. Luedecke related how Hitler had sent him to America in 1924 to obtain funds for the Nazis. When Hitler came to power in Germany in August, 1934, he awarded Ford a swastika decoration, which Ford never returned or repudiated even after war was declared. Prior to 1941, however, it was not treasonable to give aid and comfort to the Nazis.

For seven years Ford distributed Nazi-originated anti-Semitic propaganda through a newspaper he published, the Dearborn *Independent*. It was edited by his public-relations counsel, William J. Cameron, who published the *Protocols of the Elders of Zion*. These discredited forgeries, slanders against the Jews, created such indignation that many Jews filed libel suits and the Jewish community organized a boycott of Ford cars.

On June 30, 1927, Ford made a public apology to Jews, pleading that it was Cameron, not he, who had been responsible for the anti-Semitic campaign of the *Independent,* which he claimed not to have been informed about. He admitted that the slander "justifies the righteous indignation entertained by Jews everywhere toward me." Also acknowledging that the *Protocols* were proved "gross forgeries," he stopped publication of the *Independent*. The boycott against Ford cars ended.

During the twenties three consecutive Republican administrations refused to recognize the Soviet Union. Colonel Raymond Robins, wartime head of the U.S. Red Cross mission in Moscow, felt that this policy was shortsighted. He enlisted the aid of Idaho Senator William Borah and Nebraska Senator George Norris to change it, but their efforts failed.

The Hearst press, which had vastly increased its circulation with sensational headlines about the Red Peril, published "Soviet" documents indicating that Senators Borah and Norris had been paid $100,000 each by the Comintern through the Soviet ambassador in Paris. Outraged, Borah initiated an investigation that proved the documents to be forgeries.

They had been promulgated by White Russian refugees, who had also cajoled Henry Ford into paying $7,000 for forged documents. The swindlers were arrested in Germany, sentenced to jail, then expelled instead as "undesirable aliens."

In 1928 the Hearst press used more forged documents to accuse Borah, Norris, and Senator Robert LaFollette of receiving more than a million dollars from the "revolutionary" Mexican Government. Hearst was mad at Mexico for expropriating his properties there. The Senate investigated. Even the "experts" Hearst produced to validate the documents were compelled to admit that they were, indeed, forgeries.

The Red-baiting of the Hearst press only obscured the fact that there were genuine acts of disloyalty by American citizens who considered their first allegiance to Moscow, not to Washington. William Odell Nowell, a Georgia Negro who came to Detroit for an auto job, was recruited for the Communist party. In November, 1929, he was invited to Moscow with twenty-six other recruits for training and returned to further Soviet objectives as president of the American Negro Labor Congress. Moscow instructed Nowell to prepare a Negro revolt in the South to coincide with a hoped-for uprising of northern workers.

Both projects fizzled, however, because of working-class distaste for communism and black fear of white terrorists in the South. Nowell took advanced training at Lenin University but grew disillusioned with Communist tactics and quit the party. Finding himself discredited as a labor organizer, he testified against accused Communist spies for the House Un-American Activities Committee (HUAC) and was rewarded by a job with the Ford Motor Company.

When the nation fell into the Great Depression in October, 1929, with unemployment quickly soaring to a total of fifteen million, industrialists were worried by the angry mood sweeping over the country. The conservative press denounced dissenters and demonstrators against the government as Reds.

In July, 1932, angered by the failure of Congress to vote a bonus promised them, seventeen thousand desperate, jobless veterans and their families marched to Washington. Camping on the edge of the city, the Bonus Army vowed to remain until Congress passed the Patman Bonus Bill. President Hoover ordered Chief of Staff General Douglas MacArthur to evict the veterans forcibly.

The use of troops, cavalry, and tanks outraged the veterans, who threw bricks. Tear-gas shells were lobbed back. A stampede among a crowd of ten thousand injured many spectators. At bayonet point the troops forced the Bonus Army back and burned down their shacktowns. National indignation burst over the heads of Hoover and MacArthur, who were charged with "murdering veterans on the streets of Washington."

It should be noted that the *Official Training Manual* (No. 2000-25) of the U.S. Army of that day taught soldiers this definition of democracy: "A government of the masses . . . results in mobocracy. Attitude toward property is communistic —negating property rights. . . . Results in demagogism, license, agitation, discontent, anarchy."

Conservatives labeled the Bonus Army a Communist plot to provoke the calling out of troops so that the Hoover Administration could be denounced as "Fascist." But Hoover's heavy-handed blunder in antagonizing the nation's veterans counted heavily against him in the elections of November, 1932. Franklin D. Roosevelt and the Democrats were swept into office in a landslide victory, and a new era began.

The decade of the 1930s saw a sharpening of conflict between the American forces of Left and Right, intensified by hard times. Roosevelt's New Deal program sought to reform the weaknesses of laissez-faire (unrestricted) capitalism, which he blamed for the Depression. Accused of seeking to scrap the capitalist system, Roosevelt explained that on the contrary, he was seeking to save it from revolution because of its excesses. Nevertheless the Right, including most big-business leaders, regarded him as a Communist or radical whose policies amounted to "creeping socialism."

The pro-Roosevelt forces, including both liberals and leftists, tended to be sympathetic toward the Soviet Union. The anti-Roosevelt forces looked toward Nazi Germany and Fascist Italy for their inspiration. Each camp accused the other of treason to American ideals. Out of their clash would come the stormy episodes of the thirties, climaxed by the explosion of the mightiest clash of world powers in history.

9

THE
FIFTH COLUMN

The American anti-Semitic movement of the thirties was fueled from Nazi Germany. Using the Jews as a scapegoat for Germany's troubles, Adolf Hitler rode to power on a wave of anti-Semitic hatred. It was the emotional cement he used to glue together his Fascist-minded supporters overseas.

His plan for piecemeal conquest of the world by his Nazi "super-race" required that the major powers be kept passive and in awe of Germany as he took over smaller countries one by one. To assure this paralysis, he established a "fifth column" of pro-Nazi traitors or sympathizers in each country, working for Hitler's interests against their own government's.

His supporters in the United States and other countries included anti-Semites, antilabor businessmen and politicians who saw in fascism a tool for handcuffing unions, extreme right-wingers who hated democracy and wanted a dictatorship, criminal classes and racketeers who saw the Fascist movement as an opportunity to exploit gullible followers, and those German-Americans who admired and were loyal to the Fuehrer.

This fifth column was directed from Germany through various channels, with the objective of encouraging isolationism ("Keep America out of Europe's wars!"). Many prominent isolationists were sincere, patriotic Americans, some of them pacifists, who wanted to spare the United States the cost in blood and treasure of a second world war. Hitler's agents skillfully exploited this sentiment for Nazi ends.

They worked to discredit Americans who wanted to aid Hitler's victims as the Nazis swallowed Austria, the Sudetenland, Czechoslovakia, and Poland; challenged England and France; then finally attacked the Soviet Union. German propaganda spread the idea that only American Jews were behind demands to boycott Germany, help the Allies, and eventually join them.

Some big-business leaders were persuaded to look upon Hitler as the world savior of Christianity, in a struggle against "Jewish" communism and liberalism. Uneducated masses were encouraged to believe that Hitler was going to free them from "the oppression of the Jewish bankers"—despite the fact that only a tiny percentage of United States bankers were Jewish.

That was why Wendell L. Willkie, nominated by the Republican party to oppose President Roosevelt in the 1940 elections, declared, "I consider . . . every anti-Semite as a potential traitor to America." When pro-Fascist Father Charles Coughlin tried to support him in the weekly newspaper, *Social Justice,* Willkie icily repudiated him.

"I am not interested," he declared, "in the support of anybody who stands for any form of prejudice as to anybody's race or religion, or who is in support of any foreign economic or political philosophy in this country."

The extent to which the pro-Nazi movement on the American Right constituted treason or conspiracy to commit treason was a question difficult to settle while the United States was still at peace. After Pearl Harbor, however, arrests of many fifth columnists followed swiftly, particularly of those who persisted in championing the cause of Nazi Germany.

What about the Left during the thirties? American Communists, whose first loyalty was to Stalin and Moscow, were only a small minority at the beginning of the decade. Their ranks grew rapidly, however, during and following the Depression. They also exerted great influence in the militant labor movement and among the nation's liberals and intellectuals.

American Communists believed in world revolution by the working classes and in Stalin as the leader of that revolution. But Stalin, unlike Trotsky, whom he exiled and then murdered, was far less interested in world revolution than in the security of the Soviet Union. He suspected a plot by the capitalist powers of the West to destroy Russia, secretly building up Hitler's war machine for that purpose.

The major goal of Stalin's foreign policy during the thirties was to thwart that plot. He used the Comintern to help mobilize the liberal and labor forces within the democracies to press for stopping fascism as a threat to world peace. Independently, this was also the policy of American liberals, who saw Hitler as a menace not just to the Soviet Union but eventually to the United States.

Hard-core Communists fanatically obeyed every directive from Moscow and had no scruples about committing treason if and when directed. Among them were actual Russian agents, just as there were German agents among the American Fascists. But many Communists were simply "true believers"—idealistic intellectuals, socialists, and labor leaders who felt that the Soviet Union offered the only real hope of stopping Hitler.

Some Americans sympathized with Communist objectives, but not wholly; or they refused to put themselves under party discipline. Others supported the anti-Fascist movement but wanted no part of the Communists. The Comintern encouraged the organization of many "united front" groups in which "fellow travelers," as well as anti-Communist liberals and labor leaders, could wage their own fight against fascism.

The extent to which the pro-Soviet movement on the Left constituted treason or conspiracy to commit treason was even harder to determine than among the pro-Nazis. Communist policy attacked Nazi Germany up until 1938, when Hitler and Stalin signed a nonaggression pact, then divided up Poland.

American Communists were stunned but quickly fell into line by stopping all agitation against Hitler, switching the line to keeping America out of an "imperialist" war on the side of Britain and France. But after Hitler broke the pact with Stalin and attacked the Soviet Union, American Communists once more crusaded for all aid to the Allies to "stop Hitler."

It was painfully obvious that their policies were blueprinted in the Kremlin. Many disillusioned liberals and laborites dropped out of the Communist party and out of some united-front groups they controlled.

"When I'm told it's great to boo Hitler on Monday, then not to boo him on Tuesday," said one defector wryly, "I know I'm in the wrong outfit."

Pearl Harbor ended the confusion, however, by making Germany our enemy and the Soviet Union our ally along with England and France. American Communists instantly won respectability and American Fascists lost it. There were no prosecutions of American Communists for treason during World War II; there was no reason for it. Few Americans worked more energetically for an Allied victory.

The day after Hitler first seized power in Germany, an organization of American storm troopers called the Silver Shirts was organized by William Dudley Pelley. Running afoul of the law, he was convicted of a felony and given a five-year suspended sentence. In 1936 he received Nazi funds to run for President on a "Christian party" ticket.

"The time has come," he declared, "for an American Hitler and a pogrom." He promised to do away with the Department of Justice, using his Silver Shirts as an army and police force.

The goateed American fuehrer was indicted for sedition when he continued his work as a Nazi agent after the war began.

"You are a traitor to your country, the arch-Quisling of America," U.S. District Attorney J. Howard Caughran accused him, "parading under a false flag of patriotism while you stabbed your country in the back. You will go down in history with Benedict Arnold and Aaron Burr!"

Protesting that he was being persecuted "by the Jews," Pelley was found guilty and sentenced to fifteen years.

Leader of the first Silver Shirt squad of storm troopers was Gerald L. K. Smith, a pastor who gave up the pulpit to follow first Huey Long, then Pelley. Breaking with the American fuehrer, he subsequently allied himself with other leaders of the extreme Right—Coughlin, Francis E. Townsend, and William Lemke. His newspaper, *The Cross and the Flag,* urged all anti-Semitic, ultranationalist groups to unite in a single American Fascist movement for greater strength.

In September, 1940, most right-wing organizations flocked into the America First Committee, which opposed Roosevelt's policy of increasing aid to the Allies.

Smith urged his followers to be "ruthless," and according to *The New York Times,* made no secret of his intention to "seize the government of the United States." Declaring his candidacy for the Senate, he told a Detroit rally that God had ordered him to save "this glorious Republic from ruin."

Although the outbreak of war with Germany shattered the America First Committee, Smith sought to revive it in January, 1943, as an America First party to "win the peace." What this meant became clearer after the war when it was discovered that America Firsters had accepted financial support from Nazi Germany. Smith, however, was not indicted with other pro-Fascists.

James True, a virulent American Fascist of the thirties, actually patented a kind of policeman's nightstick for killing Jews. Distributing Nazi and British Fascist propaganda, he vowed, "Fascism is the answer . . . it is the last defense of Christian capitalism." He sought to further his goal by selling firearms to American Nazi groups.

The chief Nazi agent in the United States during the decade was George Sylvester Viereck, who had been propaganda adviser of the German embassy since the First World War. In a book written after that war Viereck explained, "Every propagandist drapes himself in the flag. The objective of German propaganda was . . . to strengthen and replenish Germany; to weaken and harass Germany's foes; and to keep America out of war."

When Hitler came to power, Viereck sought to use Congress itself as an agency for disseminating Nazi propaganda in the United States. Founding a publishing house called Flanders Hall, he contracted for books from congressmen who promoted isolationism, defeatism, and anti-Communist and pro-Nazi policies.

He worked out a scheme to have the American Government subsidize bulk mailings of his pro-Nazi propaganda through the office of Congressman Hamilton Fish, Sr., who had headed the first congressional committee to investigate "subversive activities" in 1930. Fish allowed his House Office Building facilities to be used as Viereck's Washington headquarters.

After war broke out, Viereck was arrested as a Nazi agent along with Fish's office clerk, George Hill, who confessed the scheme. Viereck would write pro-Nazi speeches for Fish and some twenty other congressmen and senators who were willing either to deliver them or insert them in the *Congressional Record* as "printed remarks." Viereck would then order reprints delivered to Hill, who mailed them out postage-free in bulk, in addressed envelopes bearing a congressional frank, to Fascist organizations throughout the country.

Hill testified that Fish had introduced him to Viereck and told him to collaborate with the Nazi agent. Viereck had paid Hill for these services and had also given him money to bribe congressmen into cooperating. Almost a million pieces of Nazi propaganda had been mailed at Government expense.

A grand jury ordered Fish to explain his involvement. He denied knowing that Viereck was in the pay of Hitler, calling him "an American citizen of long standing and good standing." His memory failed him in answering other embarrassing questions.

Viereck was convicted, but the Supreme Court reversed his conviction on March 1, 1943, on the technical ground that he was not compelled to report to the State Department any of his activities except as "agent of a foreign principal."

The rise of pro-Fascist agitation in the United States led the House of Representatives in 1934 to appoint a McCormack-Dickstein Special Committee on Un-American Activities to investigate Nazi propaganda. The committee uncovered a sensational Fascist plot to seize the Government that involved many captains of industry. These industrialists, horrified by Roosevelt's "Socialist" New Deal and his encouragement of a powerful labor union movement, were convinced that the capitalist system could not survive four years of "That Man in the White House."

A putsch to seize control of the Government by force was organized by pro-Fascist extremists during Roosevelt's first term. They hoped to capture the White House and establish a Mussolini-style dictatorship under distinguished war hero Major General Smedley Butler, ranking major general of the Marine

Corps. The plotters made forty-two separate efforts to persuade Butler to lead the putsch.

A war hero twice awarded the Congressional Medal of Honor, Butler was their ideal choice for a "man on horseback" because of his great prestige among American veterans, who could be expected to rally behind him as an American dictator. Gerald C. MacGuire, former head of the Connecticut American Legion, offered Butler three million dollars to form the projected new "superorganization" of veterans and three million dollars more as needed. General Butler, an incorruptible patriot, pretended to play along with the plotters to get full details of the cabal.

MacGuire explained what they had in mind once the White House was captured: "Did it ever occur to you that the President is overworked? We might have an Assistant President. The dumb American people will swallow that. We have got the newspapers. We will start a campaign that the President's health is failing." Then the new "supersecretary" of the conspiracy would move up to become "Acting President," because Vice President John Nance Garner had no wish for that office.

MacGuire informed Butler that in two or three weeks a new organization "to maintain the Constitution and so forth" would be announced in the press and would contain many names important in American industry. This was the organization behind the putsch.

"In about two weeks," General Butler testified, "the American Liberty League appeared, which was just about what he described it to be."

Contributors to the league, as revealed by the Seventy-fourth Congress, included seven members of one of the nation's major corporations, the racist president of a leading oil company, partners of Wall Street banking firms, the head of a major steel company, the former chairman of a leading food company, the director of a southern railroad, and dozens of other important figures.

General Butler now felt that he knew the whole treason plot. Roaring a furious rejection of the offer to make him an American Mussolini or Hitler, he warned MacGuire and his backers not to try to get another general for their scheme.

"My one hobby is maintaining a democracy," he snapped. "If you get a half million soldiers advocating anything smelling of fascism, I am going to get a half a million more and lick hell out of you, and we will have a real war right at home!"

He went to Washington on February 15, 1935, and testified in secret session before the McCormack-Dickstein Committee.

"The whole affair," he declared, "smacked of treason to me. . . . I have one interest in all of this, and that is to try to do my best to see that a democracy is maintained in this country." Another witness, a newspaper man, corroborated his testimony.

"MacGuire denied these allegations under oath," noted the committee's official report (No. 153, 74th Congress, 1st Session, House of Representatives), "but your committee was able to verify all the pertinent statements made by General Butler, with the exception of the direct statement suggesting the creation of the organization. This, however, was corroborated in the correspondence of MacGuire."

It added, "Evidence was obtained showing that certain persons had made an attempt to establish a Fascist organization in this country. There is no question that these attempts were discussed, were planned, and might have been placed in execution when and if the financial backers deemed it expedient."

Significantly, the American Liberty League quickly dissolved after the McCormack-Dickstein report. None of the principals involved in the plot was indicted for treason, possibly because President Roosevelt was anxious not to widen the gulf between himself and big-business leaders, whose cooperation he needed to make the New Deal work. Besides, the country was not at war, and treason would be difficult to prove—especially against the best corporation lawyers in the nation.

In 1934 a noted anti-Semite, Mrs. Elizabeth Dilling, published the first "subversive list" since J. Edgar Hoover's list of the Palmer-raid days. In a book called *The Red Network* she named such dangerous radicals as Rev. Harry Emerson Fosdick, Mahatma Gandhi, Sigmund Freud, New York Mayor Fiorello La Guardia, Sinclair Lewis, Chiang Kai-shek, Mrs. Eleanor Roosevelt, and New Deal legal adviser Felix Frankfurter.

She labeled as "Communist institutions" the Y.M.C.A., the Federal Council of the Churches of Christ, and the Civil Liberties Union. Addressing students at the University of Chicago, she accused, "You're all guinea pigs of Stalin. The University of Chicago is a Red school!"

In her book Mrs. Dilling explained that fascism "seeks a harmony between all classes," a remarkable conclusion apparently confirmed by several trips to Germany. In a lecture tour during the thirties she attacked democracy as a system of "mobocracy," explaining that the United States was not a democracy but a republic. Winning support from some right-wing congressmen, senators, and wealthy New York superpatriots, she refused to stop recruiting for fascism after Pearl Harbor. The Department of Justice indicted her as a pro-Nazi propagandist.

"I am guilty only of pro-Americanism!" she cried.

The swastika flew boldly at all meetings of the German-American Bund, organized in 1933 under orders from Berlin. Its fuehrer was Fritz Kuhn, a Munich-born Nazi-party member who had entered the United States in 1926 as a chemist in the Ford plant. The Bund had its own private storm troopers wearing swastika armbands, who were necessary, Kuhn explained, to protect Bund rallies from being broken up by Communists.

A New York legislature investigative committee, under Senator John J. McNaboe, reported that the Bund's private army was "being trained to serve . . . a foreign dictator." Kuhn's demagogic speeches mimicked Hitler's, charging that all Communists and bankers were Jews, and that 60 per cent of the Government was Jewish.

"Free America!" he cried, giving the Nazi salute.

He established twenty-four Bund camps throughout the United States with Nazi funds. Bund cells received orders from Berlin on propaganda activities, espionage, and revolutionary preparations. Their mission was spelled out by Hitler: "National Socialism would be worth nothing if it restricted itself to Germany alone and did not seal the rule of the superior race over the whole world for at least one thousand to two thousand years."

The Nazis spent an estimated $300 million a year toward this goal on their foreign auxiliaries. Returning from a visit to Germany, Fritz Kuhn wrote, "We must impel American politics with a pure German feeling. . . . America, under all circumstances, must keep out of any European war. That is the greatest service we can show Germany." A special prayer was written for the Bund's youth groups. It began, "Adolf Hitler, we believe in Thee."

The Bund distributed Joseph Goebbels's propaganda vilifying President Roosevelt and Mayor La Guardia, who was called a "Jewish lout" and "chief gangster" for suggesting that Hitler belonged in a chamber of horrors. La Guardia replied dryly that while his mother had a slight infusion of Jewish blood, "I regret that it is not enough to boast of."

Throughout the thirties, as Fritz Kuhn and others on the extreme Right urged Americans to take the Nazi road to the future, the Jews in Germany were being terrorized, thrown into concentration camps, and murdered along with political opponents and Slavic people in countries Hitler overran.

As American outrage grew at these atrocities, Kuhn stopped displaying the swastika at Bund rallies, replacing it with American flags. But on November 29, 1939, the movement received a setback when Kuhn was convicted of larceny and forgery and was sentenced to up to five years in jail. The New York legislature then passed an act forbidding the use of uniformed storm troops at rallies.

The Bund continued under Gerhard Wilhelm Kunze, an ex-chauffeur, of Philadelphia. In 1940 Bund officials were indicted in New Jersey for violating a 1935 state law against inciting racial and religious hatred. Convicted and sentenced, they appealed to the State Supreme Court. A reversal was granted on the ground that the law violated the rights of free speech because there was no "clear and present danger to the State."

The jubilant Bund held a joint rally with the Ku Klux Klan in New Jersey. The legislature thereupon closed down the Bund's Camp Nordland as a public nuisance. Florida and other states passed statutes outlawing Bund activities. The Bund nevertheless held a national convention in September, 1941.

The war put the Bund out of business. In April, 1942, the F.B.I. arrested sixty-four alien members. Many were convicted and jailed; some who were naturalized citizens lost their citizenship for disloyalty. Kunze, tried as a spy for supplying military information to Germany, was sentenced to fifteen years, with five years added for fomenting resistance to military service in the American Army.

Japan, too, had its agents operating in the United States during the thirties. Typical was Cincinnati-born John S. Farnsworth, an Annapolis graduate who had served on destroyers in World War I and commanded a Navy air-squadron base at Norfolk. After marrying a society girl, he began to live above his means and was court-martialed for refusing to pay his debts.

Unable to get civilian employment with this blot on his record, he offered his services as an aviation technical adviser to other countries. Japan was interested, but only in naval secrets he could obtain for them. Farnsworth, who held a grudge against the Navy for "persecuting" him, agreed.

Calling on old friends in naval circles, he managed to steal confidential documents from their offices. One officer's suspicions were aroused by the large bills Farnsworth was flashing around. The F.B.I., alerted, put a twenty-four-hour watch on him.

They secured evidence that he was collecting Navy code and signal books, sketches, photographs, blueprints, maps, and ship models and was meeting secretly with the Japanese naval attaché, Commander Akira Yamaki, and later with his successor, a Commander Ichimiya. Following the trail, the F.B.I. located firms that had photostated naval material for Farnsworth. This tactic had been abandoned as too risky; Ichimiya installed photostating machines in his own hotel quarters, which maids were forbidden to enter.

Through Farnsworth, eight years before Pearl Harbor, the Japanese learned the effectiveness of almost every gun in the U.S. Navy and the capabilities of its aircraft carriers.

Arrested, Farnsworth insisted that he had only been pretending to spy for the Japanese in order to penetrate their espionage network, hoping that if he succeeded, the Navy would reinstate him. At his trial in February, 1937, however, he pleaded nolo contendere—neither an admission of guilt nor a plea of innocence. Found guilty, he was sentenced to four to twenty years in a federal penitentiary.

But the most dangerous treason, as war approached, continued to be that practiced by Hitler's American admirers.

10

THE LANGUAGE
OF HATE

Another important crusader for fascism in America was Lawrence Dennis, who had worked for the State Department for seven years. Switching to Wall Street, he became a leading intellectual spokesman for the far Right. In 1936, as "an important American Fascist," he was given an interview with Mussolini, and in Germany he met Baron Ulrich von Gienanth, who financed Nazi agents in the United States. Jailed Nazi agent Friedrick Auhagen later reported having given Dennis Nazi funds.

"I do not believe in democracy or the intelligence of the masses," Dennis wrote in a book predicting the coming of American fascism. "This book is addressed . . . to the ruling groups, actual and potential." He praised German and Italian aggression in the countries they overran and Japan's rape of China.

With the outbreak of war with Germany, Dennis applied for a commission in the U.S. Army but was refused. He continued working discreetly for fascism by using important senators, representatives, publishers, businessmen, and clergymen to promote his views. When his activities came under fire from an investigative body of Congress, he did not hesitate to ask the Civil Liberties Union to defend his right to denounce democracy.

A year after Pearl Harbor he was still proposing that the Republican party speak out against the war effort and continuing to denounce the New Deal as a Communist plot.

The patriotism of some industrialists during the late thirties seemed as dubious as that of those involved in the abortive putsch plot exposed by General Butler. On November 23, 1937, when Hitler was testing his tanks and planes in Spain to overthrow that democracy for Franco's fascism, a curious meeting took place in a Boston hotel. Seven prominent American industrialists and congressmen reached a secret cartel agreement with two Nazi consul generals—Baron von Tippleskirch, of Boston, and Baron Manfred Freiherr von Killinger, of San Francisco.

They established joint monopolies of aluminum, synthetic rubber, tungsten, quinine, and other essential defense materials. The resultant shortages hampered American defense production to the point that a Senate hearing held by Senator Harry S Truman branded Standard Oil and other important corporations involved as "traitors" to the war effort. The hearings also accused many American business leaders of refusing to cooperate with the Government's request that they convert half their production to defense needs before Pearl Harbor and of balking even months afterward.

The same Nazi consul general who engineered the cartel agreement, Baron von Killinger, also blueprinted a plan for a revolutionary network to "liberate" Americans from democracy. A West Virginia engineer, George E. Deatherage, was a key figure in this conspiracy. In 1935 he had revived a defunct Ku Klux Klan organization called the Knights of the White Camellia

to spread anti-Semitism. He also founded the American Nationalist Confederation, uniting seventy-two different Fascist
groups.

Deatherage distributed propaganda shipped to him by the
Nazi bureau, World Service. He also sought to frighten American Jewry by ordering his followers to spread "terror and fear"
by burning swastikas on hills overlooking towns. When war
broke out, he withdrew from the organizations he headed to
avoid prosecution. But in February, 1942, he was fired from his
job at the Norfolk Naval Base as an "undesirable" security risk
and a year later was charged with sedition.

Another important pro-Fascist agitator was Joseph P. Kamp,
who in 1935 began editing a newspaper called *The Awakener*.
He abandoned it after two years when its virulent anti-Semitism
began to run it into trouble and organized the Constitutional
Educational League. It distributed over two million copies of a
booklet called *Join the C.I.O. and Help Build a Soviet America,*
in which Kamp charged that labor's sit-down strikes in Detroit
were a Moscow-directed plot for revolution.

The Senate Civil Liberties Committee, headed by Senator
LaFollette, began investigating the league. Kamp accused the
committee of being "disloyal and un-American." Through his
league, which had industrial support, he was instrumental in
getting the House of Representatives to set up a new Un-American Activities Committee "to investigate subversion" under his
friend, Martin Dies of Texas. It soon became clear that HUAC's
target would be almost exclusively the Left, not the Right.

Edward Sullivan was appointed chief investigator of the Dies
Committee. In addition to a record of nine police arrests and
employment as a labor spy, he had directed a Fascist Ukrainian
group, edited an anti-Semitic hate sheet, and been a speaker at
German-American Bund rallies.

HUAC's second chief investigator was Dr. J. B. Matthews,

whose writings were reprinted by the Nazi Foreign Office and who wrote in his autobiography, "America's answer to communism will be fascism." Years later Matthews became a close adviser of Robert Welch, founder of the John Birch Society.

When Dies took over HUAC in May, 1938, Congressman Dickstein, who had headed HUAC in the earlier investigation of the Fascist conspiracy exposed by General Butler, declared, "One hundred and ten Fascist organizations in the United States have had, and have now, the key to the back door of the House Un-American Activities Committee."

Three congressmen—Coffee, of Washington, O'Toole, of New York, and Hook, of Michigan—accused Dies of making HUAC "a sounding board for the un-American Fascist groups." Several congressmen charged that Gerald L. K. Smith was the secret director of HUAC.

"It seems to me," said Congressman Savage of Washington, "that all Gerald L. K. Smith has to do is yell 'sic 'em,' and the committee's counsel takes after whatever party Mr. Smith is peeved at."

The Dies Committee attacked New Deal projects, the National Labor Relations Board, the Department of Labor, the Workers' Alliance, and the American Youth Congress as "Communist-infiltrated." To charges that he was trying to silence the Left and help the Right, Dies replied, "What amendment in our Constitution protects these spies and agents of foreign governments?" HUAC produced political headlines, but no spies.

The Imperial Wizard of the Ku Klux Klan praised Dies, declaring that his program "so closely parallels the program of the Klan that there is no distinguishable difference between them." When Dies left Congress in 1945, he admitted to a St. Louis *Post Dispatch* reporter that his primary purpose had been to harass the New Deal by charges of Communist infiltration, which he knew were hurting the Roosevelt Administration.

A national poll in 1934 declared the second most powerful and popular man in the country, after Roosevelt, to be Father Charles E. Coughlin, the "radio priest." At first he supported the New Deal, thinking it would bring "social justice" modeled after Mussolini's corporate fascism. He soon found Roosevelt's policies too liberal for his tastes. When the President appointed some prominent Jews to public office, the anti-Semitic Coughlin turned against him fiercely.

Through radio broadcasts, his weekly paper, *Social Justice,* and mass rallies at which he made demagogic speeches, Coughlin peddled the Nazi line. When he attacked Roosevelt as "the great liar and betrayer . . . the Scab President," his bishop forced him to make a public apology.

In the 1936 elections he joined Gerald L. K. Smith and Francis Townsend in supporting Congressman William Lemke's Union party against Roosevelt. "One thing is sure . . . democracy is doomed!" he cried out on his radio program. "This is our last election. It is fascism or communism. We are at the crossroads. . . . I take the road of fascism!"

Lemke received only 900,000 votes, but Coughlin's National Union for Social Justice soon had almost 8,500,000 members. In 1938, he urged all Fascist groups to join in a "Christian Crusade against Communism." The result was the Christian Front, which used strong-arm squads and aspired to put in power a corporate-clerical state like Franco's.

Social Justice served as the Front's mouthpiece against what Coughlin called the "poppycock of democracy." He filled it with liberal quotes from Hitler's and Goebbels's anti-Semitic speeches; articles by George Sylvester Viereck, the registered Nazi agent; and even the forged *Protocols of the Elders of Zion.*

The Catholic Church made it clear that his views did not represent Church policy, and many prominent Catholic leaders denounced him. But Coughlin persisted in broadcasting Nazi propaganda, charging that it had been necessary for Hitler to take power to keep the Jews from communizing Germany, then the world. Meanwhile the Christian Front's street gangs grew more and more violent in breaking up anti-Fascist meetings.

Mayor La Guardia ordered the New York Police Department to crack down, and 233 of the Front's storm troopers were arrested in 1939. Seventeen members of the Front were indicted for conspiring to mount a Fascist revolution to take over the Government. The prosecution accused them of seeking to "incite Jews to riot and then have a revolution and a counter-revolution." The jury disagreed, and the Fronters went free.

Coughlin was finally silenced on the air by his ecclesiastic superiors in 1940. He continued to publish *Social Justice,* however, even after Pearl Harbor. In April, 1942, the Attorney General banned it from the mails as "a systematic and unscrupulous attack upon the war effort."

As Coughlin's star faded, American Fascists found a new hero in Charles A. Lindbergh, the "Lone Eagle," who had become an American idol in 1927 by making the first nonstop solo flight over the Atlantic. Tall, blond, handsome, and modest, married to an ambassador's daughter, "Lucky Lindy" had been lionized everywhere. The whole nation had sympathized when a brutal kidnapping had cost his son's life, impelling him to take his family to live in England.

In 1938, Lindbergh made a trip through Europe, visiting Germany, the Soviet Union, and France. Returning to England, he joined appeasers in that country who insisted that Germany's air power was superior to that of the British, Russians, and French combined. Outraged Britons accused him of trying to frighten the Western powers into appeasing Hitler.

"Those who are favored with his views," reported the *London Express,* "say that he never hesitates to voice his glowing admiration for Hitler and the German State." Eleven noted Soviet fliers who had been Lindbergh's hosts in Moscow charged, "He had an order from English reactionary circles to prove the weakness of Soviet aviation and give Chamberlain an argument for capitulation at Munich."

When Lindbergh returned to Germany, Hermann Goering enthusiastically decorated him with the Service Cross of the German Eagle as a "distinguished foreigner who has deserved well of the Reich." Supporters of Lindbergh later insisted that he had only been ingratiating himself with the Nazis under orders of the U.S. Defense Department to gather intelligence for them on Nazi air strength, a claim never validated.

On April 25, 1941, President Roosevelt compared Lindbergh to a Civil War Copperhead for his isolationist stance. Lindbergh resigned his commission in the Air Force Reserve. Several months later, addressing a nationally broadcasted America First Committee rally, he parroted the Fascist line:

> The three most important groups who have been pressing this country toward war are the British, the Jews and the Roosevelt Administration. . . . [The Jews'] greatest danger to this country lies in their large ownership and influence in our motion pictures, our press, our radio and our government.

The New York *Herald Tribune* accused him of having "sinned against the American spirit." Secretary of the Interior Harold Ickes asked sarcastically whether anyone had ever heard Lindbergh speak on behalf of democracy. William Allen White characterized his speech as "moral treason."

A controversial and tragic figure now scorned and denounced as a traitor by the majority of shocked and saddened Americans who had once idolized him as a great national hero, Lindbergh lapsed into brooding silence. One cynical radio wit asked, "What's everybody mad at Lindy for? He only followed Adolf's advice that if you're going to tell a lie, tell a whopper if you want to be believed. Look where it got Adolf!"

Once war was declared, however, Lindbergh's supporters saw to it that he was given some secret flying missions in the South Pacific, for which he was awarded the Congressional Medal of Honor and restored to the Air Force Reserve as a general.

John Roy Carlson, an anti-Fascist investigator who infiltrated the Fascist movements of the thirties, reported on a typical rally of the American Nationalist party. About four hundred people had crowded into a New York ballroom for the occasion.

"The whole country is overrun with foreigners, niggers, Jews," yelled a speaker. "Is this the white America of our fathers? Is this a land of Christian patriots or blood-sucking Communists? This here country has been stolen from us Christians by a bunch of conniving rats. What are we going to do about it?" The mob burst into an uproar.

"Kill the Jews! Hang them from lampposts!"

"Wipe every atheistic Communist off the face of the earth!"

Another speaker shouted, "Democracy, democracy, democracy! They throw it in our faces. You hear it on all sides till you get sick of it. What is this democracy? It is a rotten form of weakness." He called for an end to "absurd propaganda against Germany." The mob enthusiastically applauded mentions of Father Coughlin, Hitler, and Franco.

The American Nationalist party organized a storm-trooper unit that taught the use of clubs, blackjacks, brass knuckles, and alley-fighting. Its recruits were part of the goon squads that joined the Christian Front to terrorize anti-Fascists.

The Front also enlisted the American Patriots, led by anti-Semite Allen Zoll, who applied unsuccessfully for a job as a Japanese propaganda agent. When New York radio station WMCA refused to carry Coughlin's inflammatory broadcasts,

Zoll threw an American Patriots picket line around the station. Offering to call it off for $7,500, he was indicted for extortion.

Another prominent Christian Front group was the Christian Mobilizers, led by Joe McWilliams, who declared, "I'm going to have the greatest collection of strong-arm men in the city. And if anybody tries to stop us . . . they'll think lightning hit them." His followers included convicts, rapists, burglars, and street toughs, who did not hesitate to assault police.

"This is another revolution," McWilliams shouted at one street meeting. "It's a revolution against the Jew first, then against democracy, then against the Republican and Democratic parties. Both are rotten . . . useless. We are going to drive them both out and . . . run this country with an iron hand, the way Hitler runs Germany. . . . We are his fellow-fighters."

The Christian Mobilizers crusaded against passage of the Lend-Lease Act, defense appropriations, and the Selective Service Act as "Jewish plots." McWilliams confessed to John Roy Carlson, "I don't believe half of this anti-Jew stuff I preach, but . . . it's the only language they understand—the language of hate. Hitler made it work and that's what I'm trying to do."

Another group known both as the American Fascists and Crusader White Shirts was led by a Tennessee fanatic named George W. Christians. He advocated seizing power by a military march to surround government buildings and "by sheer numbers and a patriotic appeal" to force officials to yield.

One night when President Roosevelt was expected in Chattanooga, Christians threatened to cut off the city's electric power. "Lots of things can happen in the dark," he hinted.

Most of the paramilitary groups in the Christian Front had plans for sabotage in the event of war with Germany. "In time of war we are all saboteurs," declared James Banahan, commandant of a secret Fascist Iron Guard unit disguised as the Midtown

Sporting Club of New York. "We'll blow hell out of this country. We'll blow up docks, power plants, ships, bridges. . . . They'll blame the Communists. We'll spread confusion and chaos. . . . If they catch you with guns, we are members of the National Rifle Association, catch on?"

Banahan renamed his group the American Phalanx and affiliated it with the Ku Klux Klan. In January, 1940, the F.B.I. arrested seventeen members, charging them with conspiracy to overthrow the Government. Tried in Queens, New York, then a strong center of Coughlinites, they were acquitted by a jury. Queens Borough President George U. Harvey defended the Christian Front as "Americans."

One of the most active workers in the American Fascist movement was Mrs. Leslie Fry, a paid Nazi agent. She worked with Baron von Killinger as West Coast organizer of the plot for a Fascist putsch. When it failed, she fled to Germany before the F.B.I. could seize her. In 1942 she made the mistake of trying to reenter the country on a German ship and was taken into custody and indicted for sedition.

The Christian Front had its friends in Congress. Representative Jacob Thorkelson considered Joe McWilliams a "staunch American" and inserted in the *Congressional Record* quotations from many Fascist and anti-Semitic sources. He praised Hitler and Mussolini on the floor of Congress and scoffed, "There is not one democracy which has survived for any length of time."

Senator Robert Reynolds, chairman of the Senate's Committee on Military Affairs before Pearl Harbor, cooperated with American Fascist leaders and inserted their propaganda in the *Congressional Record*. As a military expert, he assured Americans that they were fortunate to have between them and the Soviet Union the protection of the islands of Japan.

Strong support for the extreme Right came from the Committee for Constitutional Government. Organized in 1937 by publisher Frank E. Gannett, it was headed by the same Edward Rumely who had been jailed as a secret German agent during World War I. The committee raised $210,000 to propagandize America First's policies. When the Senate Committee to Investigate Lobbying Activities called Rumely to testify in 1938, he removed his name from the organization's stationery.

William E. Dodd, America's ambassador to Germany from 1933 to 1938, warned Americans, "A clique of U.S. industrialists is hell-bent to bring a fascist state to supplant our democratic government and is working closely with the fascist regimes in Germany and Italy."

Attorney General Jackson, speaking at the Boston Club on October 16, 1938, enumerated the names of the leading Fascists in America. The two largest press associations in the nation, the United Press and the Associated Press, reported the speech but for reasons best known to themselves omitted all the names except one. Boston's *Law Society Journal* published all.

Two months later Secretary of the Interior Harold L. Ickes followed Jackson's warning with a speech at Columbia University naming Lawrence Dennis as an American propagandist for fascism and Lindbergh and Coughlin as the nation's leading quislings—Vidkun Quisling was a Norwegian fifth columnist who had betrayed Norway to the Nazis.

After war was declared, Ickes attacked the big business firms that had sabotaged America's defense needs because of cartel agreements with I. G. Farben, the German firm controlled by Hitler. He pointed out that for over four months Alcoa had resisted expanding production of aluminum, depriving the country of the equivalent of ten thousand fighter planes. "If America loses the war," he said in June, 1941, "it can thank the Aluminum Corporation of America."

In May, 1940, British sympathizers in America rallied behind William Allen White in a Committee to Defend America by

Aiding the Allies. That September, the isolationists and pro-Fascists united their forces in the America First Committee.

America First argued that the new world war was none of America's business, and that the United States should simply ignore it. After the war it was discovered that America Firsters had accepted financial support from Nazi Germany. Pearl Harbor exposed the bankruptcy of America First's insistence that American interests were not threatened by the spread of international fascism, and the organization collapsed.

Meanwhile, what about subversion on the left?

11   "AS CLOSE TO TREASON AS I DARE"

The Communist party grew stronger through the thirties by appeals designed to attract not only the working classes but also the intellectuals of America. New members were often recruited into the party through personal friendships.

The celebrated black novelist Richard Wright was a case in point. As a lonely young man in Chicago, he found a welcome in the Communist John Reed Club. White Communists showed him that they had no color bias, respected his talent, and were willing to form personal friendships with him.

"How different this was," he marveled, "from the way in which Negroes were sneered at in America. . . . I was meeting men and women . . . who were to form the first sustained relationships in my life."

It became an "in" thing for intellectuals to sympathize with the Reds, giving rise to the label of "parlor pinks." As during the sixties, radicalism on campus was a mark of distinction among the brightest members of the student body and faculty. This new left wing fully supported Roosevelt's New Deal as the first mild measures of social reform.

Many law-school graduates and other intellectuals flocked to Washington to work enthusiastically for the New Deal. Some of these civil servants were Soviet sympathizers; many were simply anti-Fascist; others were influenced toward the left by friendships with men they admired.

Whether some were disloyal, advancing the interests of the Soviet Union over those of the United States, was a question that would eventually be raised with dramatic consequences. Many government officials later accused by rightists of "treason" had sinned only in being active anti-Fascists before Pearl Harbor had made it patriotic. On the other hand, many American isolationists attacked by leftists as "Hitler agents" were actually only intent upon keeping America out of war.

Cooperation of fellow travelers with the Communists in anti-Fascist activities began to fall off in 1936, when Stalin began the strange Moscow trials of alleged Soviet traitors. For two years top Soviet officials accused themselves of monstrous acts of treason in open court and were led away to firing squads. Shocked American anti-Fascists suspected that the confessions had been procured by torture or threats to the defendants' families. Repelled by Stalin's paranoiac idea of "justice," they withdrew from cooperation with U.S. Communists.

The American League Against War and Fascism, which represented a whole range of anti-Fascist sentiment from middle-of-the-road Democrats to Communists, fell to pieces in 1938 when Hitler and Stalin signed their nonaggression pact. American anti-Fascists wanted no part of a world leader who was willing to "shake hands with the devil" and join with him in invading and dividing Poland.

During the two years between the Hitler-Stalin Pact in August, 1939, and Hitler's attack on Russia in June, 1941,

American Communists tried to close their dwindling ranks. Their speakers used Marxist rhetoric to justify the pact, urging an end to aid to the Allies and a new isolationism.

"We must have faith in the great Soviet Union as the only Socialist power in the world!" cried one party member at a 1940 streetcorner meeting witnessed by the writer. "Stalin has foiled the plot of the capitalists to drive Germany against Russia and has taken eastern Poland to protect the Polish people under a Socialist shield."

"That wasn't your line *last* year!" someone yelled.

"Stalin explained that dialetic materialism requires Communists to be flexible, according to the needs of changing events," the speaker replied. "The true enemies of working people everywhere are the imperialists of Wall Street and Ten Downing Street. Stop our rotten capitalists from dragging us into a dirty war! Down with Roosevelt, who has betrayed the New Deal to the munitions-makers who want blood money!"

Those Communists and fellow travelers who remained committed to the party during this period were almost wholly those who continued to have faith in Stalin, like Ossip Garber. A Bronx photographer, he was found to be operating a passport-forging ring for the use of Communist agents traveling abroad and was sentenced to prison for two years.

But as the war drew closer, the counterespionage branch of the F.B.I. concentrated on the major threat to American security—Hitler's spies and seditionists. Early in 1940, William Sebold, a naturalized American visiting his family in Germany, was picked up by the Gestapo and detained until he agreed to train and serve as a Nazi spy. Returning home, he set up a short-wave radio transmitter in a house at Centerport, Long Island, operating a clearing-house for coded military information brought to him by other Nazi spies.

But Sebold was no traitor; he had notified the F.B.I. of the plot. The station was under the control of G-men, who fed Sebold misleading facts for transmission to Germany in code. Nazi spies who brought Sebold military secrets were photographed by a concealed camera. One spy bragged of having sold information on a top-secret U.S. bombsight to Germany for four thousand dollars. In June, 1941, the F.B.I. suddenly moved, and thirty-three men and women were arrested, cracking the major Nazi espionage ring in the United States.

With war an imminent possibility, in June, 1940, Congress passed the Smith Act, making it unlawful to advocate or teach the overthrow or destruction of the Government by force or violence or to be part of any group advocating such doctrine. Rightist lawmakers who pushed the bill intended it for use against the extreme Left, not the extreme Right.

But war with Germany brought consternation to the forces of the Right. To persist in pro-Fascist, antiwar efforts was now, by the Constitution, open treason. The Fascist movement either became inactive or went underground. The few pro-Fascists who continued their activities were arrested.

HUAC, under Martin Dies, nevertheless persisted in searching for traitors only on the Left. President Roosevelt condemned the committee. Vice President Henry Wallace compared Dies to Goebbels. The F.B.I. called HUAC's reports fake. Congressman Eliot, of Massachusetts, accused Dies of playing into the hands of the enemy and undermining the war effort. Letters poured into Congress demanding the abolition of HUAC, but Dies stubbornly insisted that the only real menace to an America at war with fascism was "communism."

Colonel Robert M. McCormick, powerful publisher of the Chicago *Tribune,* was an ardent supporter of rightist causes from the Dies Committee to America First. Together with his cousin, Joseph Patterson, publisher of the New York *Daily News,* and Patterson's sister, Eleanor Patterson, publisher of the

Washington *Times-Herald,* McCormick published daily items that were regularly used by Joseph Goebbels for Nazi propaganda.

Congressman Elmer J. Holland denounced the McCormick-Patterson papers in the *Congressional Record* as "the vermin press," whose aim was "to preach defeatism among our civilians and mutiny among our soldiers, to spread dismay among our allies, and to create joy in the hearts of our enemies."

Three days before Pearl Harbor the Chicago *Tribune* published a secret war-prospectus prepared by the Army and Navy Joint Board, outlining America's defense plans in case of war. The paper's headlines indicated that the plans proved the President's intention to drag America into the war against Germany. Secretary of War Henry Stimson was outraged.

"What would you think of an American General Staff," he asked Americans, "which in the present condition of the world did not investigate and study every conceivable type of emergency which may confront this country, and every possible method of meeting the emergency? What do you think of the patriotism of a man or a newspaper that would take those confidential studies and make them public to the enemies of this country?"

On April 17, 1942, Librarian of Congress Archibald MacLeish accused some publishers of treason without naming them. One publisher, MacLeish revealed, had told his staff that he intended to come "as close to treason as I dare." The American Society of Newspaper Editors was urged not to cross the line "where freedom of expression darkens into treason."

William Allen White, influential editor of the Emporia *Gazette,* called it a good speech, "but I wish he had named names—Coughlin, McCormick, Patterson, Pelley, et al."

"MacLeish," declared Colonel McCormick, "is a Communist." Conservative publishers called MacLeish's attack an attempt by the Roosevelt Administration to silence its critics.

Attorney General Francis Biddle urged the Senate Judiciary Committee to permit military censorship because "the most closely guarded military secrets of the government have come into the possession of newspapers and magazines and ultimately into the hands of agents of enemy governments." Among secret material leaked to Nazi Germany and Japan in this way, Biddle revealed, had been aircraft data, maps of Midway Island naval installations, Army codes, classified Navy communications, and photographs of Army camps and airfields.

The three McCormick family papers, undeterred even after Pearl Harbor, published a list of ships participating in the Coral Sea Battle against Japan. The dispatch carried a Washington dateline and quoted unnamed Navy officials as sources. The Administration angrily took the publishers to court for betraying military secrets to Japan.

Pleading not guilty, the Chicago *Tribune* admitted that their list had really been compiled in Chicago from a book on ships, with no information from the Navy. The case against the three papers was dismissed, but Congressman Holland called the two Pattersons "America's number-one and number-two exponents of the Nazi propaganda line . . . doing their best to bring about a Fascist victory." Radio Berlin sympathized with the McCormick-Patterson press as victims of "Roosevelt's dictatorship."

Some important industries were also unwilling to cooperate with the war effort. Most of Detroit's auto firms resisted the Government's demands that they convert their production to defense needs. Standard Oil explained that its cartel agreement with I. G. Farben of Germany prevented its manufacture of synthetic rubber in the United States.

"This is treason!" Senator Harry S Truman said angrily.

The War Production Board accused the Carnegie-Illinois Steel Corporation of refusing to fill Government orders needed for shipbuilding while diverting iron and steel to favored customers for civilian use. President Roosevelt ordered the Navy to take over three plants of the Brewster Aero Company for refusing to cooperate with the Government's aviation needs.

Diehard pro-Fascists continued their hate campaigns against the Government even after Pearl Harbor.

In March, 1942, Edward Holton James, of Massachusetts, circulated a leaflet charging that the President had "plotted wars against nations which had done us no harm." He demanded Roosevelt's resignation and a peace bid to the Axis powers.

Awaiting trial for criminal libel, he declared, "I have no use whatever for this thing called democracy. . . . We should have storm troopers just like Hitler did. They must be brutal. . . . The only way to save America is for Hitler and Japan to smash us." He disseminated a series of *Grapevine Letters* urging the organization of seditious "Yankee Minute Men" groups.

"Of course I know the *Grapevine Letters* conflict with the law," he confided to John Roy Carlson. "And I know what it means if we're caught. But I'm within my constitutional rights in putting them out. It's the sedition laws which are unconstitutional." In January, 1943, he wrote a *Grapevine Letter* assailing President Roosevelt for provoking the war with Japan and in March declared, "He who resists the draft today, in the name of liberty, gains a place of honor by the side of the immortal heroes who founded this country."

Kurt Mertig, a Hamburg-American Line employee, continued to call meetings of the Citizens Protective League he had founded to promote the Fascist line. "This is nothing more than a Roosevelt war," he told followers one night. "All your money is being turned over to the Reds and the British." He blamed "the traitor congressmen and senators who passed the Lend-Lease Bill. They are traitors to America."

The meeting was also addressed by Mrs. Leonora Schuyler, an anti-Semitic superpatriot who had "revealed" that the Pope was

Jewish when the Vatican had condemned Hitler. She defended Japan as "the only civilized nation in the Orient."

Mertig was ordered removed three hundred miles inland by the Army in 1942 under the Relocation Order allowing the Secretary of War to exclude security risks from coastal regions.

Another war protester was Francis P. Moran, head of the New England Christian Front, who worked out of an office he claimed to use for "sociological research." His office was closed down by the F.B.I. in November, 1942, and he was summoned before a Washington grand jury for writing in a leaflet: "Mr. Roosevelt has sent our citizens to their death. He is guilty of murder. . . . We advocate the refusal of all sincere and courageous American citizens to pay such taxes."

The war effort, said the President, "shall not be imperiled by a handful of noisy traitors . . . who in their hearts and souls have yielded to Hitlerism and would have this republic do likewise." But when the F.B.I. arrested three men for "alleged seditious utterance," they were released by order of Attorney General Francis Biddle.

"At this time," Biddle explained, "every reasonable attempt should be made to maintain both free speech and public safety. . . . Freedom of speech should be curtailed only when public safety is directly imperiled." It was an interpretation of the "clear and present danger" concept which sought to protect the right of dissent. If a citizen could not depend upon his guaranteed rights under the Constitution, what was to distinguish American democracy from its foe, German fascism?

The released pro-Fascists jubilantly called an antiwar rally, stating in leaflets: "The U.S. Attorney General says we have a PERFECT RIGHT to talk—AND WE WILL!"

Likewise, when the West Virginia State Board of Education sought to enforce a "patriotic" state law compelling school children to salute the American flag, Supreme Court Justice Robert

H. Jackson wrote the majority opinion in 1943 (*West Virginia v. Barnette*) finding the state law in violation of both the First and Fourteenth Amendments.

"If there is one fixed star in our constitutional constellation," Jackson declared, "it is that no official, high or petty, can prescribe what shall be orthodox in politics, nationalism, religion or other matters of opinion, or force citizens to confess by word or act their faith therein."

The F.B.I. tried to follow Biddle's guidelines in distinguishing disloyalty from dissent. It was not always easy.

The National Workers League was a Nazi-front organization seeking to erode morale among defense workers in vital war industries. It held rallies and flooded Detroit with pro-Fascist propaganda. Its secretary, Garland L. Alderman, wrote a letter published in the May, 1942, issue of *The American Mercury,* promising, "The peace will be negotiated by Hitler, Mussolini, the present Japanese Government, and by Sir Oswald Mosley of England, and by patriotic Americans such as General Moseley, William Dudley Pelley, Father Coughlin, Colonel Lindbergh and Senator Nye."

Alderman managed to avoid indictment for sedition but made the mistake of leading a mob of twelve hundred people armed with knives, clubs, and guns against Negroes moving into a federal housing-project. He was arrested for complicity in rioting.

Frank W. Clark, of Tacoma, a former lieutenant in Pelley's Silver Shirts, sought to build an underground army of pro-Fascist veterans armed with guns and knives. He used false names and letter drops to throw F.B.I. agents off his trail.

"When the day comes to settle the score and I'm given a reward for my patriotism," Clark said, "I want to be made chief executioner of those guys who are now sticking up for democracy." He worked closely with socialite Mrs. Lois de Lafayette Washburn, who insisted that Japan was not really America's enemy but its ally, "helping us fight off the Jew and the Jewish capitalist system." Both Clark and Mrs. Washburn were arrested by the F.B.I. for sedition on January 4, 1943.

In Utah, a religious fanatic and racist from South Africa, Ernest Hollings, headed the Christian party. Proclaiming Hitler "the Redeemer of the American Constitution," he called for reversing the war to ask Germany and Japan to send troops to the United States to help fight "American communism."

Ralph Townsend, a former consular official, was editor of *Scribner's Commentator,* which had been the voice of the America First Committee. Indicted for sedition, he fled, was caught, and confessed to being an unregistered paid propaganda agent for the Japanese. The magazine was shut down. Its publisher, Douglas Stewart, went on trial for perjury in a District of Columbia court in March, 1947.

Baron von Strempel testified that he had authorized Hans Thomsen, of the German embassy, to pay Stewart over ten thousand dollars to spread Nazi propaganda throughout the United States. Thomsen's testimony confirmed this. The jury nevertheless acquitted Stewart, possibly because the Cold War was now raging.

One dramatic case of treason involved a twenty-two-year-old lens grinder named Herbert Haupt, son of a naturalized German inmigrant who was an ardent Nazi. Joining the German-American Bund and training weekends at a Nazi youth camp in Michigan, young Haupt enjoyed swaggering around in uniform. In 1941, to escape the draft, he fled to Germany.

In June, 1942, a German submarine put ashore two rubber boats on American beaches—one near Amagansett, Long Island, the other near Jacksonville, Florida. Each had a quartette of Nazi saboteurs with enough explosives to blow up bridges, tunnels, shipping locks, and defense plants. Herbert Haupt was part of the second squad.

One nervous saboteur lost his nerve and sought to save his

skin by tipping off the F.B.I., making a full confession. Both squads were quickly rounded up before they could do any damage. Haupt was arrested at his parents' home in Chicago.

Five days later President Roosevelt appointed a secret military commission to hear the case. Haupt and the other seven defendants confessed, but their attorney argued that they had not committed a single act of sabotage and had not intended to. They had agreed to be Nazi agents, he claimed, only to escape from Germany and join friends and relatives in America.

"To accept the version of the defense, gentlemen," the judge advocate general told the eight officers on the commission, "is to conclude that the defendants came here not as invaders but as refugees." The verdict was life imprisonment for one defendant, thirty years for another, and death in the electric chair for Haupt and the others. They were executed at noon the same day and were buried in unmarked graves in Washington.

Haupt's father, Hans Max Haupt, was tried for "harboring an enemy of the United States." Convicted of treason, he was freed on appeal to the Supreme Court, which decided that the Government had not proved his guilt fully enough to satisfy constitutional requirements. Ruled the Court: "The law of treason makes, and properly makes, conviction difficult, but not impossible."

The saboteur who had been sentenced to thirty years, a naturalized American named Anthony Cramer, also won his freedom on appeal because only one and not two witnesses, as required by the Constitution, had testified to his treason.

By eight months after Pearl Harbor, under the direction of Attorney General Biddle, Hoover's F.B.I. had arrested and brought to trial a total of 9,405 Axis agents, both American- and foreign-born. One of the first sent to jail was Laura Ingalls, an aviatrix who had been an America First agitator. Found to be a paid but unregistered Nazi agent, she told the Court, "My motives were born of a burning patriotism and a high idealism. . . . I am a truer patriot than those who convicted me!"

Another American who sabotaged the war effort was Robert Jordan, Harlem's self-styled "black fuehrer." Employed as a sailor on a Japanese steamship line, he had organized the Ethiopian Pacific Movement, Inc., pledging its support to both Japan and Hitler. Embittered by American racism, he opposed fighting a war against Japanese "blood brothers of color."

"If American Negroes looked ahead," he declared, "they would fight for the interest of Japan, the leading dark nation." At street rallies in Harlem he promised that Japan would liberate the black man, and urged Negroes to organize a fifth column against the Government. Indicted for sedition, he was sentenced to ten years in federal prison.

Early in 1942 a Nazi flier who was a prisoner of war in Canada escaped to Detroit with the aid of Max Stephan, a Detroit Nazi and America Firster. Charged with treason for supplying the escapee with money, clothing, and shelter, Stephan was sentenced to death.

John Eoghan Kelly, Christian Front organizer and promoter of Franco's brand of fascism in the United States, was indicted as a paid Franco agent in May, 1943, and convicted.

The Department of Justice indicted Mrs. Washburn, Frank W. Clark, Mrs. Leslie Fry, George Deatherage, and two others for sedition on January 4, 1943. Senator Nye, whose isolationism had led him into America First, declared, "They are no more guilty than I am." The charges against them, he insisted, were invalid because they were based upon the defendants' antiwar activity before Pearl Harbor.

Senator Robert A. Taft, of Ohio, agreed that the "indictments present a real danger to the continuance of freedom." McCormick's Chicago *Tribune* called the proceedings a "Moscow propaganda trial." The trials began on July 2 and continued through 1944. Five years after the first indictments, the Justice Department was still trying to collect enough evidence to convict them of wartime treason. In November, 1946, Chief Justice

Bolitho L. Laws, of the Circuit Court of Appeals, finally ordered dismissal of the indictments against sedition defendants who had not yet been convicted.

The end of the war left an important category of obvious traitors still to be tried—those Americans who had been out of the reach of the Department of Justice because they had committed their treason from the lands of the enemy.

12

DAY OF RECKONING

Once the war was won, traitors who had been helping the enemy war effort from abroad were sought by the Government. The most prominent were those who had broadcast Axis propaganda from Berlin, Rome, and Tokyo, seeking to demoralize American servicemen. They were often frustrated failures, misfits in their native land, who combined spite against the United States with enjoyment of power, comfort, and status in the service of the enemy.

Robert H. Best, an eccentric 220-pound southerner who dressed in high-laced boots and a Stetson, had been a foreign correspondent for the United Press in Vienna. He had stayed away from his own country so long, veteran correspondent William L. Shirer suggested in his book *Traitor,* that Best had lost touch with American thinking and been infected with the Nazi virus. When his dispatches became more propaganda than news, United Press ordered him home. Best procrastinated until he was fired for "insufficient work and performance."

After Pearl Harbor Best had been rounded up with over a

hundred American correspondents and diplomats who were interned at Bad Nauheim. The Nazis quickly singled him out for preferred treatment, however, giving him comfortable quarters in a hotel and fine meals. When the internees were repatriated as a group in May, 1942, Best chose to stay behind.

He began broadcasting propaganda for Goebbels, exalting Hitler as "a crusader for civilization" and trying to persuade G.I.s preparing to invade Hitler's "Fortress Europe" that they were fighting the wrong enemy. Captured when American forces overran Germany, Best came to trial in Boston in 1948.

He testified that he had never meant to betray his countrymen, only to warn them against the dangers of "bolshevism, Jewry and Roosevelt's warmongering." Found guilty on all charges, he was sentenced to life imprisonment. He declared defiantly, "If I had to do it again, I would!"

One of the more astonishing traitors to be arraigned was the influential poet Ezra Pound. Idaho-born, the red-bearded eccentric, who wore long hair before it was fashionable and dressed in Byronic collar and long-flowing cape, was arrested in Genoa in the spring of 1945. Pound had lived as an expatriate in Italy. He had detested pre-Mussolini Communist disorders in the cities and admired the dictator as an apostle of law and order.

He had also been naïvely impressed by the racist views of a German economist, Silvio Gesell, that all a country's economic troubles were caused by "usurious interest rates extracted by Jewish money lenders." Over Radio Rome, Pound made prewar speeches urging Americans not to support any war against Mussolini or Hitler, because it was a "Jewish plot."

When Pearl Harbor was attacked, Pound sought to return home but found his request for aid in being repatriated coolly ignored. Enraged, he went on Radio Rome to denounce the war, praise "Hitler the martyr," and urge Americans to accept the Fuehrer and Mussolini as their true leaders.

After the war he was imprisoned in a Pisa detention camp, then flown to Washington in February, 1946. Found mentally unfit for trial, he was sequestered in St. Elizabeth's Hospital, Washington, D.C., as insane. Many Americans who respected his poetic talents were deeply upset by this judgment, even though they deplored his treason and knew he could be executed for it.

"I believe he should be freed," Ernest Hemingway said in 1954, "to go and write poems in Italy, where he is loved and understood." He labeled Pound's treason "errors of judgment and pride."

Another celebrated postwar trial was that of "Axis Sally," whose real name was Mildred Gillars. Maine-born, she was an actress, singer, and radio announcer so spectacularly unsuccessful that she had subsisted on crackers and apples for months. In a desperate attempt to win publicity, she had faked a suicide attempt after first notifying the press.

Unable to "make it" in the United States by her twenty-eighth birthday, she had left for Europe to try her luck there. In Germany she had formed an attachment to Max Otto Koischwitz, a former naturalized American who had taught German literature at Hunter College. Mildred imbibed his anti-Semitic, anti-Roosevelt, anti-British theories, and he got her a job at the *Rundfunk* radio station as a broadcaster of news overseas.

As Axis Sally, her voice was soon familiar to G.I.s in England, who were preparing to invade occupied France. She sought to destroy their morale by describing vividly the horrible fate that awaited them. D-Day, she warned, stood for "doom, defeat, and death." When they were fighting bloodily on Omaha Beach, she taunted them with doubts about the fidelity of the wives and sweethearts they had left behind in America.

After Germany's defeat, Axis Sally sought to escape into the Russian zone of occupation but was captured and brought back to the District of Columbia for trial. She protested that she couldn't be tried for treason, because she had sworn an oath of allegiance to Nazi Germany, making her German. But she could produce no proof. The jury found her guilty, fined her ten thousand dollars, and imposed a sentence of from ten to thirty years.

Her counterpart in the Pacific, "Tokyo Rose," was actually not one woman but as many as twenty who assumed the role. Only one was an American citizen—Iva Ikuku Toguri, of Los Angeles, who had been educated at the University of California. She had been visiting a dying aunt in Japan in 1941 when war broke out. The Japanese had offered her repatriation in the fall of 1942, but she had refused to go.

News from the United States revealed that 110,000 Americans of Japanese ancestry were being evacuated from their homes on the West Coast and sent to relocation centers inland as security risks. The evacuation was being carried out under General John DeWitt, who had declared, "A Jap is a Jap and must be wiped off the map."

Outraged that Japanese-Americans were being deprived of their rights as citizens, with no charges of any kind being filed against them, simply because of their ancestry, Iva felt no desire to return to a concentration camp. She later claimed that she had asked the Japanese to intern her, but they had refused. Instead, in 1943 she had gone to work for Radio Tokyo, broadcasting to American G.I.s in the Pacific.

Like Axis Sally, her propaganda on the Tokyo Rose show was designed to make American soldiers discouraged, homesick, worried that their wives and girl friends back home were untrue to them, and fearful they would never get home alive. The bait used to lure G.I.s to listen was popular music.

Introducing records, she would say cheerfully, "Enjoy them while you can, because tomorrow at 0600 you're hitting Saipan . . . and we're ready for you. So while you're alive let's enjoy. . . ." After the battle of Leyte Gulf she purred, "Orphans of the Pacific, you are really orphans now. With all your ships sunk, how will you get home?"

In 1945 Iva married a Portuguese-Japanese employee at the Domei Japanese News Agency, Felipe D'Aquino. When she was apprehended and tried in a Federal District Court in 1949, she pleaded that this marriage canceled her American citizenship, but Chief Judge Michael J. Roche ruled out the plea because she had made treasonous broadcasts before the marriage.

Found guilty, she was sentenced to a ten-thousand-dollar fine and ten years' imprisonment. Released after serving seven years, Iva fought payment of the fine, claiming she had been unfairly convicted because of anti-Japanese prejudice. She also alleged that she had been made a scapegoat by the Japanese Government for some of the Radio Tokyo broadcasts made by other Tokyo Roses because she was the only American.

She was not without her defenders among Pacific veterans she supposedly had subverted during the war. The writer recalls listening to her one time in the jungles of New Guinea when a fellow G.I. said, "We ought to write Tokyo Rose a fan letter. She sure plays great music. Makes you homesick, all right, but it passes the time real nice. And that bunk she peddles is always good for laughs. Besides, with no women around, that sexy American voice is sure nice on the ears!"

If Iva had accepted repatriation during the war, she would undoubtedly have been compelled to join other Japanese-Americans herded in camps situated in arid sections of the West. Hastily constructed, these centers were surrounded by barbed-wire fences, armed guards, and night-time searchlights—in effect, prison compounds. Shortages of food and medical supplies touched off a riot at one center.

A 1944 Supreme Court decision (*Korematsu v. U.S.*) had upheld the Government's right to move the Japanese-Americans

inland as a security measure, although dissenting Justices
Roberts, Murphy, and Jackson called it unconstitutional. The
War Relocation Authority was warned, however, that it could
not detain any person whose loyalty had been established.

The War Department set up registration procedures to "clear"
loyal Japanese-Americans so that they could leave the centers.
Those seventeen or over were asked, "Will you swear unqualified
allegiance to the United States of America . . . and forswear
any form of allegiance or obedience to the Japanese Emperor?"

The question was an intolerable affront to thousands of
American-born citizens of Japanese descent, who resented the
slur on their loyalty. Some had fought in the American Army
during World War I. Others were second- and third-generation
Americans (Nisei and Sansei) with as little as one-sixteenth
Japanese ancestry.

They knew that a similar oath was not being required of the
Kamps, Deatherages, Kuhns, Vierecks, Pelleys, McWilliamses,
Trues, and other pro-Fascists, some of them German-born and
avowed Hitlerites, who were allowed at liberty. For that matter,
why weren't all Americans with German and Italian ancestry
also being herded into concentration camps as security risks and
compelled to take loyalty oaths? The Japanese-Americans could
see only one explanation—racial discrimination against Asians.

"I will not forgive this government of the United States as long
as I live," vowed one outraged Japanese-American. "Does the
Government think we are without pride?"

Some thirty-one thousand internees took the oath, but over six
thousand flatly declared themselves disloyal in protest. Many of
these were older Japanese-Americans who had been compelled
to sell their homes, farms, and businesses in California at a
heavy loss and now had nothing to go back to after a lifetime of
hard work in the country of their adoption. Deciding to return to
Japan after the war, they made it necessary for their respectful

American-born sons and daughters to choose family loyalty over loyalty to country.

About three thousand refused to register for military service, torn with doubt or embittered by unfair treatment. "We are Americans, not dual citizens," argued one Nisei. "But if we are citizens in the first place, then why are we in these camps?"

In January, 1943, however, the War Department decided to accept volunteers from the camps for all-Nisei combat units. The Nisei resented the "opportunity" offered them to serve their country, not as other young Americans did, but in a segregated Nisei command. The reason, apparently, was to isolate them to control any possible sabotage or treason. Many Nisei, nevertheless, swallowed their pride and enlisted.

Their units proved among the bravest and best American troops in the war, achieving an outstanding war record that did much to erase anti-Japanese prejudice after the war.

Some Japanese-Americans who renounced their citizenship in anger cooled off after the war and sought to compel the Government to restore their status. The War Department, they charged, had subjected them to unfair intimidation and coercion. In some cases citizenship was restored. In others no clear-cut decisions were reached, leaving them, as one Nisei wryly described their status, "native American aliens."

Among genuine traitors the Government caught up with after the war was Jane Anderson, of Georgia. A pro-Fascist newspaperwoman, she had covered the Spanish Civil War not only as a reporter but also as a spy for Franco. Caught by the Loyalists, she had been tried and sentenced to death but was saved by the intervention of the U.S. State Department.

In Berlin when Pearl Harbor was struck, she was hired by the Nazis to make short-wave propaganda broadcasts to America four times weekly over the *Rundfunk* under the pseudonym of

Lady Haw Haw. The name derived from the nickname for William Joyce, Lord Haw Haw, another American traitor broadcasting to England for the Nazis.

In April, 1942, Lady Haw Haw made a bad tactical blunder. Seeking to paint a rosy picture of life under Hitler even after years of war, she broadcast a description of delicious meals being served in Berlin's cabarets. America's OSS (Office of Strategic Services) decided that front-line Nazi soldiers on field rations and rationed Germans in the countryside would also enjoy hearing how well the German 4-F's and bureaucrats were eating and enjoying the war back in Berlin.

So they translated her English broadcast into German and re-broadcast it to Germany and Nazi battle areas. Goebbels, apopleptic with rage, threw Lady Haw Haw off the air as a fool. The Department of Justice had declared her a traitor, but after the war the indictment against her was dropped because her brief fiasco as a Nazi propagandist didn't seem sufficiently important to be worth prosecuting as treason.

Lord Haw Haw was another matter, but one which the British handled. Fifteen days after Britain and France went to war with Germany, English short-wave listeners began to hear him speaking in impeccable British tones from Berlin. He described every German victory ecstatically, praised the power of Hitler's air force, and warned the Allies to sue for peace at once or face certain doom.

The owner of the beautiful British voice was not a British subject but an undersized, ugly, awkward American named William Joyce. His father, Irish-born contractor Michael Joyce, was a naturalized American citizen whose son had been born in the United States in 1906. Three years later the family moved to Ireland. Influenced by his father's antipathy to the Irish independence movement, at fifteen William Joyce served as a spy for the British Black-and-Tans. The Joyce house was burned down.

In 1922, when Ireland won her freedom, the Joyces left for England, where William attended Birkbeck College for Working Men at London University.

After graduating, he sought to become a British Army officer but was rejected because of doubts about his citizenship and also because in both appearance and lineage he did not pass muster with the officer class of "gentlemen." He joined the Conservative party but found the same social rejection.

Bitterly convinced that England was in the "wrong hands," he turned to Sir Oswald Mosley's British Union of Fascists, dedicated to making England a dictatorship. Although he became Mosley's deputy and propaganda director, Joyce was stung when Mosley, too, refused to accept him as a social equal.

Breaking with Mosley, he founded his own National Socialist League, looking to German rather than British fascism. In 1939, as war with Germany loomed, Joyce applied for a British passport and left for Berlin, determined to help Hitler conquer the England that had snubbed him. When Britain declared war, Joyce joined the *Rundfunk* as Lord Haw Haw.

Several times daily he delivered Nazi-colored newscasts so skillfully that Germany decorated him for his services. In 1940 he was granted German nationality. D-Day came as a shock to him, crumbling his dreams of returning to England as a deputy fuehrer. As Hitler's empire collapsed, Joyce fled Berlin disguised as a German but was caught and flown to England to stand trial as a traitor on September 17, 1945.

His lawyers decided to defend him on the ground that he was actually an American citizen by birth and therefore could not be tried as a British traitor. "It will be amusing to see if they get away with it," he said. The prosecution insisted that, American or not, Joyce had claimed and received the protection of a British citizen by applying for a British passport. He therefore owed allegiance to the Crown.

The jury agreed, and Joyce was hanged as a traitor on February 1, 1946. Ironically, had he sought an American passport to go to Germany from England, the British would not have been able to try him for treason. And since he had accepted German naturalization before America entered the war, he would also have been immune to American prosecution.

The American and British postwar trials for treason were models of restraint compared to the hunger for revenge that swept over countries that had been invaded and kept under the Fascist heel during the war. In 1946, the French, purging citizens who had turned collaborationist during the Nazi occupation, arrested half a million men and women on charges of treason. Holland had 130,000 such arrests; Belgium, 60,000.

In France many suspected traitors were given "street justice" by enraged mobs who shaved the heads of women who had associated with Nazi troops, and beat and shot male collaborators. Thousands were executed in mass trials.

In 1946 *Time* marveled at the strange phenomenon that had led hundreds of thousands of people to betray and seek to destroy the institutions under which they had lived. "In the twentieth century," *Time* observed, "treason has become a profession, and its modern form is the betrayal of ideas."

In the United States the discredited and battered Right thirsted for revenge against the liberals and the Left. Swiftly changing world events restored their influence in Congress, and the pursuit of treason on the Left was soon in full cry.

13

"TWENTY YEARS OF TREASON"

Even before the war ended, it became apparent that there would be a postwar struggle between the Soviet Union and the West for spheres of influence in Europe and the Pacific. The question of which side would replace the power vacuum left by the downfall of fascism in Europe and Japanese imperialism in Asia resurrected the anti-Communist movement in the West.

All through the war, enthusiasm for the Russians had been considered not only respectable but patriotic. Thousands of American leaders of Congress, industry, labor, education, the arts, and the military, including General Douglas MacArthur, lauded the heroism of the Red Army and the Russian people. Even Joseph Stalin, despite the infamous Moscow trials and the blood of millions of anticollective kulaks on his hands, was hailed as a great wartime Allied leader.

American celebrities socialized extensively with Russians visiting or stationed in the United States. In Hollywood many movie stars attended parties given by Russian film producer

Boris Moros, unaware that he was not only a spy for the Soviet Union but also a double spy for the F.B.I., reporting on stars suspected of being Communist-party members.

What had been patriotic and popular from December, 1941, through August, 1945, quickly became subversive after the war. Americans who continued to express Soviet sympathies after March 12, 1947, when President Truman enunciated the Truman Doctrine to contain Russian expansionism, risked investigation for disloyalty.

A revived American Right began to attack the Government once more, this time accusing it of harboring a Communist conspiracy that had brought about the downfall of Generalissimo Chiang Kai-shek by Mao Tse-tung. The architect of this "treason," the Right insisted, was Secretary of State Marshall.

During the war both Chiang's Nationalists and Mao's Red Army were ostensibly allied forces fighting, with American aid, against Japan. But American General Joseph ("Vinegar Joe") Stilwell, in charge of American forces in Southeast Asia, had reported angrily that while Mao's forces fought superbly against the Japanese, Chiang's army was inactive and corrupt, using American aid only to enrich themselves and fight Mao's guerrilla forces. Asian experts in the State Department, after investigation, recommended that Chiang's aid be cut.

In 1949 Chiang's forces were overthrown by Mao's Red troops, mostly with arms captured from the Japanese and in battles with the Nationalists. Chiang withdrew to the island of Formosa. Still subsidized by extensive American aid, he paid for a "China Lobby" to agitate Congress in his behalf against mainland China under Mao. Pressure by the Pentagon silenced General Stilwell upon his return, so that he could not tell the press the truth about Chiang.

The China Lobby cooperated with American rightists in seeking to pin a label of treason on all who had opposed or criticized Chiang. John Stewart Service, an anti-Chiang State Department official who had served in China during the war, was arrested in 1945 under the Espionage Act. He was accused of revealing to Philip Jaffe, editor of *Amerasia,* an American magazine critical of Chiang, classified information submitted to the State Department on the Chinese situation. A Washington grand jury voted unanimously against his indictment.

However, Jaffe and two other Asian experts were indicted and fined for "illegal possession of government documents." The New York *Herald Tribune* observed, "The State Department's action in calling in the FBI and bringing about arrests which resulted in headlines concerning 'spies' and 'espionage' was an extreme action."

A Senate subcommittee investigation headed by Senator Millard Tydings reported, "We have considered the evidence and concluded that John Stewart Service is neither a disloyal person, a pro-Communist, nor a bad security risk." But in December, 1951, with McCarthyism raging, a Presidential Loyalty Review Board found "reasonable doubt as to his loyalty," and Service was dismissed.

During the late summer of 1945, Igor Gouzenko, a twenty-six-year-old Russian cipher clerk with the Soviet embassy in Canada, decided to defect. He took with him files documenting a Russian spy ring in the West. As a result of his disclosures, twenty persons were arrested and eleven sent to prison.

The most important contact Gouzenko named was Dr. Allan Nunn May, British nuclear physicist, who had provided the Russian military-espionage apparatus, G.R.U., with a steady stream of nuclear information after the first atomic bomb was dropped on Japan. May, who had strong Communist sympathies, felt that the Soviet Union was entitled, as a war ally, to share in Allied nuclear research for its own protection. An even balance of nuclear power, he believed, would preserve world peace after the war by keeping the West from threatening nuclear warfare against the Soviet Union.

Placed on trial, May admitted his treason, explaining, "I only embarked on it because I felt this was a contribution I could make to the safety of mankind. I certainly did not do it for gain." Found guilty of communicating information that might be useful to an enemy, he was sentenced on May 1, 1946, to ten years in prison. He served six of them.

Gouzenko's exposure of a spy ring heightened the Red scare in the United States. Politicians began seeking subversives in every aspect of American life—schools, Hollywood, the universities, Government, the Army, labor unions. Americans who had been anti-Fascist before the war, cooperating with the Soviet Union as a war ally, now found themselves smeared indiscriminately as "Commie traitors."

In 1945 Representative John E. Rankin, of Mississippi, whom *Newsweek* called "a militant racist and anti-Semite," took over the chairmanship of the old Dies (HUAC) Committee. He won headlines with a Red probe of Hollywood involving top stars. Full credit for the investigation was claimed by Gerald L. K. Smith, described in 1948 by the Illinois American Legion as "probably the most vicious of the rabble-rousing and sensational hate-mongers operating today."

Eight years later when Smith sought to campaign for Nixon, he was told, "There is no place in the Republican party for the race-baiting merchandisers of hate like Gerald L. K. Smith."

During the next two years Rankin, aided by New Jersey Representative J. Parnell Thomas, used HUAC to mount political attacks against American liberalism. They ran the committee as a kind of public court-martial, branding prominent Americans as traitors without giving them the right to cross-examine accusers and paid informers.

In 1946, when OPA Administrator Chester Bowles announced

a price ceiling for the 1946 cotton crop, Rankin denounced him as a Communist. HUAC's chairman called the Fair Employment Practices Committee "the beginning of a Communistic dictatorship the like of which America never dreamed."

The postwar rise of the extreme Right in the United States was helped by Stalin's intransigence in retaining control of East Europe behind what Churchill labeled an Iron Curtain. When Secretary of Commerce Henry Wallace criticized the Cold War drift of American foreign policy under Secretary of State James Byrnes, President Truman requested Wallace's resignation, indicating that anticommunism was now the order of the day.

But Truman's new hard line toward the Left did not placate the Right, which now attacked the Democratic Administration as having been "soft on Communism" and "riddled with traitors." In the elections of November, 1946, they won control of both houses of Congress. Rankin demanded that a commission be set up to probe and fire every government employee whose loyalty was "found to be in doubt."

In March, 1947, to placate the Republican Congress, Truman issued a Loyalty Order subjecting two million federal employees to a purge of suspected Communists or fellow travelers, at a cost of twenty-five million dollars. That same year, ironically, in a congressional study called *Fascism in Action,* Representative Wright Patman, of Texas, found the real danger to American security still the threat of the extreme Right:

> We are forced to admit that fascism is today an ever-present danger to our democracy. . . . $100,000,000 per year is donated to propaganda organizations, some of which show very definite fascist tendencies. . . . Many persons feel that all agreements between American firms and foreign firms should be made public. This would automatically expose attempts of foreign fascists to work through American sympathizers.

He quoted Dr. Douglas M. Kelley, a noted psychiatrist who had attended the Nuremberg Trials of Nazi defendants:

> We can find the same ideas thinly veiled in our public press today. Even worse, we find some of our top political men, members of our highest governing bodies, making statements which would do credit to Rosenberg, Hitler, or Goebbels. . . . I am convinced that there is little in America today which could prevent the establishment of a Nazi-like state.

But HUAC and the loyalty probe operated solely on the premise of the "Red Menace." Under Truman's Loyalty Order, 570 civil-service employees were fired and 2,478 forced to resign. In the first two years of the Eisenhower Administration, with Senator Joseph McCarthy leading the witch-hunt, over 8,000 more government employees left public service.

The loyalty probes extended everywhere—into the armed forces, universities with government research grants, plants with defense contracts. On the most dubious circumstantial evidence —often "guilt by association" or on the word of paid informers with prison records—thousands of Americans were forced out of their jobs under a cloud of suspicion about their loyalty. Many were State Department officials who had been identified with our wartime pro-Soviet policy.

When one federal employee challenged the legality of his dismissal, the Supreme Court refused to overturn a lower court verdict against him, in effect upholding the constitutionality of Truman's Loyalty Order (*Friedman v. Schwellenbach*, 1947).

In October, 1947, Thomas initiated a new probe into Communist infiltration in Hollywood, guaranteeing front-page headlines for HUAC. Proceedings were halted to allow testifying right-wing stars such as Adolph Menjou, Gary Cooper, George

Murphy, and Ronald Reagan to pose for movie, TV, and newspaper cameras. One of HUAC's committeemen was Richard M. Nixon, a new, young Republican representative from California.

Writers labeled Communists in the hearings sought to appear before HUAC to defend themselves against charges made against them, but were not allowed to make statements. Film writer Dalton Trumbo pointed out that Gerald L. K. Smith had been allowed to make a statement.

"That statement is out of order," Thomas snapped.

Several indignant writers who refused to be silenced were removed forcibly from the hearing. As he was dragged off, Trumbo shouted, "This is the beginning . . . of American concentration camps!" The mother of film star Ginger Rogers had testified earlier that Ginger had refused to speak the "subversive" line of a Trumbo script in a wartime film: "Share and share alike—that's democracy."

"The most un-American activity in the United States today," said a Detroit *Free Press* editorial, "is the conduct of the congressional committee on un-American activities."

"Neither Mr. Thomas nor the Congress," reminded the Republican New York *Herald Tribune,* "is empowered to dictate what Americans shall think." Under the pressure of intense press criticism, Thomas reluctantly let the next Hollywood writer testifying make a statement.

Albert Maltz accused HUAC of not permitting persons named as Communists to cross-examine witnesses who made the charges. Denouncing HUAC's bias, he cited a statement Thomas had made linking the New Deal with the Communist party and describing the Ku Klux Klan as "an acceptable American institution." He wound up with scornful defiance:

If I were a spokesman for General Franco, I would not be here today. I would rather be here. I would rather die

than be a shabby American, groveling before men whose
names are Thomas and Rankin, but who now carry out activities in America like those carried out in Germany by
Goebbels and Himmler.

Some of the hostile Hollywood witnesses were known Communists or former Communists; some were fellow travelers;
some were simply liberals. But all argued that it was unconstitutional to compel them to reveal their political affiliations or
beliefs, past or present. Ten refused on principle.

Maltz reminded HUAC of Thomas Jefferson's declaration
that all Americans had the right to hold and maintain whatever
opinion they chose—"which shall never be a crime in my view;
nor bring injury to an individual."

Famous novelist Thomas Mann, a refugee from Nazi Germany, warned in November, 1947, against political inquisitions
under the pretext of anticommunism: "That is how it started in
Germany. What followed was fascism, and what followed fascism was war." But that month Thomas won citations for contempt of Congress against the "Unfriendly Ten" writers.

The Motion Picture Association of America held a secret
meeting in New York at which producers agreed to fire the Ten
and blacklist them from further employment. Sued by the
writers, five years later four major studios made out-of-court
settlements of $107,500 for breach of contract, conspiracy to
blacklist, and damages for loss of employment.

On December 7, 1947, the Ten were tried on contempt
charges. Five received the maximum sentence, a year in jail and
a one-thousand-dollar fine; two got six months in jail and a five-
hundred-dollar fine. Ironically, HUAC's chairman went to jail
before any of them did. In 1948 Drew Pearson revealed that
J. Parnell Thomas had put his relatives on the public payroll, accepting kickbacks for this nepotism. He was tried and sentenced

to up to eighteen months in the Federal Correctional Institution at Danbury.

The Red hunt went on under other leaders, with little or no protection for the rights of persons whose reputations were impugned. After the press was given the names of 110 teachers summoned to appear before HUAC for interrogation, the hearings were never held, leaving the named teachers under a cloud of suspicion. Accusations were made on the basis of paid informers such as Manning Johnson, who had admitted publicly that he would commit perjury "a thousand times over" for the F.B.I.

Witnesses frightened by HUAC into incriminating others were praised as patriotic. Some former Communists, disillusioned with the party, turned informer for HUAC and the F.B.I., naming government officials they accused of being involved in a Soviet espionage system.

Connecticut-born Elizabeth Bentley, who drifted into the Communist party out of hatred for fascism in the 1930s, became the mistress of Jacob Golos, head of World Tourists, Inc., a front for Soviet espionage operations. When Golos died in 1943, Miss Bentley continued to act as courier between American spies and N.K.V.D. (Soviet secret police) agents.

Growing disenchanted with the party as a Moscow puppet, she went to the F.B.I. in August, 1945. Two years later, having continued in the party as an F.B.I. operative, she testified before a New York grand jury that she had collected party dues from secret party members working for the Office of Strategic Services, the Department of Commerce, the Air Corps, and the Treasury.

HUAC sought fresh headlines by summoning Miss Bentley to testify before the committee. She named a number of government officials as Communist-party members. Nathan Gregory Silvermaster, an Agriculture Department official during the war, was labeled a spymaster whose influence with Lauchlin Currie, a Roosevelt adviser, had enabled him to place Communists in government jobs. Silvermaster called Miss Bentley a "neurotic liar," branding her charges "false and fantastic."

He exercised his right under the Fifth Amendment to refuse to answer questions that might tend to incriminate him.

Miss Bentley accused Harry Dexter White, Assistant Secretary of the Treasury and author of the Morgenthau Plan, of giving Silvermaster classified information for the N.K.V.D., relayed through her. White, ailing in health, accused HUAC of star-chamber proceedings (secret, unfair trials). He died shortly afterward of a heart attack.

Lauchlin Currie admitted having known Silvermaster and others accused by Miss Bentley but denied involvement with anyone he knew to be a Communist.

Another Government witness, Whittaker Chambers, senior editor on *Time* and a former Communist, named Alger Hiss as a member of a prewar Communist apparatus in Washington. Hiss was a high-echelon official in the State Department, an ardent New Dealer, and adviser to President Roosevelt at Yalta. He had been made Secretary General of the U.N. Organization at San Francisco under Truman and had become director of the Carnegie Foundation for Peace. Chambers's accusation created an uproar, and the issue quickly became a political one.

Administration supporters, believing in Hiss's innocence, lined up against New Deal haters, who saw in the Hiss case powerful proof of their charge that it had harbored Communists.

Philadelphia-born Chambers had drifted into the Communist party in 1925, convinced that Lenin had the right idea about gaining power to build a just society. He had worked as an editor for the *Daily Worker* and the *New Masses*. In 1932, he was told by a Russian agent that he had been selected for underground work, and was used as a courier of secret messages.

In 1934, J. Peters, Russian head of the underground in the United States, had introduced Chambers as "Carl" to Harold Ware in Washington. An adviser to the Department of Agriculture, Ware, like Peters, was a Comintern agent. His job was to organize important American Communists in the Government into a Red cell under his control. One secret member of the Ware group, Chambers alleged, was Alger Hiss.

Hiss, who had once been secretary to Supreme Court Justice Oliver Wendell Holmes, had joined the Socialist party during the Depression years. He had gone to Washington to join other bright young Harvard lawyers working for the New Deal at the urging of his friend Lee Pressman, a lawyer with the AAA (Agricultural Adjustment Administration). His brilliance was quickly recognized, and his career began to soar.

What happened subsequently was a matter of controversy. According to Chambers's testimony, Hiss was brought into the Ware group through Pressman but did not attend gatherings to avoid suspicion. He received his orders from the Comintern through Chambers, who would give him State Department documents to microfilm for transmission to Moscow.

In May, 1939, shaken by the Moscow trials and having broken with the Communist party, Chambers decided to expose the Ware ring. He confided in anti-Communist writer Isaac Don Levine, who brought him to Assistant Secretary of State Adolf Berle. Berle had promised to investigate the matter, Chambers testified, but nothing had been done.

Berle later contradicted Chambers. "This was not, as he put it, any question of espionage," Berle testified. "There was no espionage involved in it. He stated that . . . a study group of some sort had been formed. . . . He did not make the direct statement that any of these men were members of the Communist party." Chambers was also shown to have given perjured and contradictory testimony.

There was reluctance to believe the word of a self-confessed former Red spy and informer against highly respected American officials, even after Chambers gave his testimony before HUAC. On August 5, 1948, Hiss voluntarily appeared before HUAC to deny every word of Chambers's allegations, stating that he had never even heard of Chambers until the previous year when the F.B.I. had asked whether he knew him.

Representative Richard Nixon was not satisfied, however, and insisted on additional HUAC hearings at which he was an active interrogator. He believed Chambers's story. Democrats accused Nixon of persecuting Hiss in order to advance his political career with Red-baiting headlines, a technique that had won him election to Congress over Helen Gahagan Douglas.

President Truman contemptuously dismissed Chambers's charges of a Red plot against America among highly placed government officials as a "red herring," pressed by HUAC as a political issue for the forthcoming 1948 elections.

In subsequent hearings it developed that Hiss had known Chambers but under another name. As each man testified in turn, their stories clashed constantly. Someone was obviously lying. In a dramatic face-to-face confrontation, Hiss finally challenged Chambers to repeat his story outside the hearing-room so that he could be sued for libel. Chambers, after some hesitation, did so, and Hiss sued.

On new evidence produced by Chambers to support his story, HUAC reconvened a grand jury, which indicted Hiss for perjury under oath before the committee. At the trial Chambers produced purloined State Department papers and microfilm he claimed to have obtained from Hiss. He had hidden them in a hollowed-out pumpkin on his farm, he had explained, and had forgotten about them. Hiss denied that he had been the one to give Chambers what were now famous as "the Pumpkin Papers."

The F.B.I. located an old 1938 Woodstock typewriter, once

owned by Mrs. Hiss, on which some of the stolen documents had apparently been copied. The defense held that the typewriter had been given away by the Hisses before the purloined documents had been copied on it, and that some documents had been stolen from Hiss's office. Hiss's attorney labeled the whole case a political stunt to hurt the Democrats.

The baffled jury could not agree on a verdict after five tries, and the case had to be tried again. By that time Chambers had dug up new witnesses, and so had Hiss. Nineteen character witnesses took the stand to vouch for Hiss's loyalty, veracity, and integrity. Hiss's lawyers introduced psychiatrists who testified that Chambers was "a psychopathic personality" whose symptoms were evidenced in repetitive lying, withholding the truth, and pathological accusations.

But the prosecution produced Republican Senator John Foster Dulles, who had helped make Hiss president of the Carnegie Endowment Fund. Dulles contradicted five different statements Hiss had made at the trial. Other witnesses backed up Chambers's testimony. The jury found Hiss guilty, and on January 25, 1950, he was sentenced to five years' imprisonment.

Secretary of State Dean Acheson, commenting on the case, declared, "I will not turn my back on Alger Hiss." Republicans charged that this proved that the Democrats were "the Party of Treason."

Nixon, who had played a leading role in the investigation and prosecution of Hiss, declared, "I think the entire Truman Administration was extremely anxious that nothing bad happen to Mr. Hiss. Members of the Administration feared that an adverse verdict would prove that there was a great deal of foundation to all the reports of Communist infiltration into the Government during the New Deal days."

Years later he said, "Looking back, I suppose the great lesson of the Hiss case is the personal tragedies involved for both Hiss and Chambers. . . . Both were, I think, sincerely dedicated to the concepts of peace and the concept of bettering the lot of the common man, of people generally. They were both idealists. Yet, here are two men of this quality who became infected with Communism . . . willing to run the risk, as they did, of disgrace in order to serve the Communist conspiracy."

Nixon's success in putting Hiss behind bars catapulted him into national prominence. He won the Republican nomination for Vice President in 1952 under Eisenhower, who introduced him to the National Convention as "a man who has shown . . . an ability to ferret out any kind of subversive influence wherever it may be found, and the strength and persistence to get rid of it." Nixon campaigned warning that a Democratic victory would bring "more Alger Hisses, more atomic spies," and attacked the Democratic candidate, Adlai Stevenson, for having been a character witness for Hiss.

Alger Hiss served forty-four months at the federal prison in Lewisburg, Pennsylvania. Released, he went quietly to work in New York as an office-supply salesman for a stationery company. He continued to assert his innocence and his belief that his name would eventually be cleared. Whittaker Chambers died in July, 1961, a bitter, enigmatic figure to the end.

The Hiss-Chambers case was only the beginning of a Republican attack on Democratic liberalism for what Senator Joseph McCarthy began calling "twenty years of treason."

14   CLIMATE OF FEAR

            The mounting tensions of the Cold War, inflamed by the testimony of former Communists like Chambers and Elizabeth Bentley, led to the indictment of eleven top leaders of the Communist party in January, 1949, on charges of violating the Smith Act by conspiring to teach the overthrow of the Government.

    The nine-month trial was a stormy one. In violent outbursts, the defendants accused Judge Harold Medina of "railroading" them to prison on Government orders. All were convicted and ten received five-year jail sentences.

    The extreme Right was well pleased with the new political climate in which treason was now found only on the Left. In 1948, Allen Anderson Zoll set up the National Council for American Education, dedicated to censoring "subversive" textbooks and demanding loyalty oaths from school and university faculties. Once described by Senator Estes Kefauver as "a notorious hatemonger," Zoll had formerly headed the American Patriots, cited as Fascist by former Attorney General Biddle.

143

Zoll's council worked closely with HUAC in mounting an investigation of "academic treason." The fallout produced the 1949 New York State Fineberg Law, and similar laws in other states, requiring the firing of any teachers who uttered "treasonable" or "subversive" words. "Is it all right," one teacher asked, "to quote the Declaration of Independence?"

The National Education Association found that by July, 1949, twenty-two states were requiring loyalty oaths, and a dozen states had fired teachers for "disloyalty—undefined." When J. B. Matthews, HUAC's chief investigator, left the committee, he took with him a suspect list of three thousand teachers, one thousand clergymen, and half a million other Americans, which he turned over to Republican Senator Joseph McCarthy, of Wisconsin.

McCarthy, ex-chicken farmer, ex-Marine, and part-time lawyer, was an unpleasantly aggressive but effective demagogue looking for a headline-winning crusade that would advance his political fortunes. He stumbled upon it in a speech he made on the Hiss case at Wheeling, West Virginia, in February, 1950.

"In my opinion," he declared, "the State Department . . . is thoroughly infested with Communists. . . . The Secretary of State proclaimed his loyalty to a man guilty of what has always been considered as the most abominable of crimes—of being a traitor. . . . It awakened the dormant indignation of the American people."

When he found his attack widely quoted, McCarthy began wildly attacking all Democratic leaders, accusing them of "twenty years of treason." He called President Truman a "——— who ought to be impeached." He made a practice of holding up a piece of paper dramatically for news photographers, intoning, "I have in my hand a list of two hundred and five names that were known to the Secretary of State as being members of the Communist party and who are still working and shaping policy in the State Department."

He never showed the list and often cited a different number of names. Senator Millard Tydings, of Maryland, summoned McCarthy before a Senate subcommittee and demanded that he reveal his list. McCarthy stalled, then finally submitted a list that had abruptly shrunk from 205 to 4 names. And he no longer charged that they were "Commoonists" or "card-carrying Commies," but simply "pro-Communist." Only two worked for the State Department. Next day he offered four more names, but only one was a State Department employee.

Senator William Benton accused McCarthy of having "borne false witness and deliberately and repeatedly corrupted facts." McCarthy countered with a libel suit, meanwhile continuing his campaign of character assassination and smear by innuendo that gave rise to a new term for irresponsible accusations against innocent people—"McCarthyism."

Describing the McCarthy inquisition, Gustavus Myers wrote in *The History of Bigotry in the United States:*

> McCarthy himself was to insult and defame Presidents Truman and Eisenhower, Cabinet officers, generals, ambassadors, fellow Senators and Americans from every walk of life. Nor was the extent of the witch hunt restricted merely to the activities of Senator McCarthy. A spirit of fear and dread blanketed the nation, and everywhere "little McCarthys" sprang up to accuse, threaten and terrorize their fellow countrymen.

Even the man General Eisenhower had called the greatest American of his century, General George Marshall, commander of the U.S. Army in World War II and Secretary of State under Truman, was described by McCarthy as part of a "conspiracy so immense and an infamy so black as to dwarf any previous such venture in the history of man."

McCarthy found no treason on the extreme Right, where American Fascists flourished in the anti-Communist hysteria he

whipped up for them. The anti-Communist Korean War provided the emotional climate in which his attacks thrived.

Harvey Matusow, a professional Red-hunter for McCarthy,
described how they mounted a headline-winning crusade against
"subversive" books:

> McCarthy's plan was simple and also dramatic: take a
> book, show that a Communist sold it to a Communist in a
> Communist bookstore, or a bookstore located in a school
> declared Communist by the Attorney General . . . and in
> that way convince all who were watching the TV show that
> the sale of such books was one of the reasons that 500,000,-
> 000 Chinese were now living under a Communist Govern-
> ment.

As a result of McCarthy's crusade, U.S. information libraries
overseas were ordered to remove books that did not meet with
his approval. In Indiana, a lady member of the State Textbook
Commission demanded the banning of all books about Quakers
as Communist because "they don't believe in fighting wars." She
also sought to ban Robin Hood, explaining, "There is a Communist directive in education now to stress the story of Robin
Hood. They want to stress it because he robbed the rich and gave
to the poor."

The Rockhill (South Carolina) *Herald* gleefully suggested
that undoubtedly the real name of the folk hero of Sherwood
Forest had been "Robinoff Hoodski." The present-day Sheriff of
Nottingham, England, observed derisively, "Robin Hood was no
Communist. She's undoubtedly thinking of Little Red Riding
Hood."

As head of the powerful Permanent Senate Subcommittee on
Investigations, McCarthy played to the TV cameras and made
headlines in rightwing papers by denouncing as "Comsymps"

(Communist sympathizers) leading Democrats, Republicans, and Protestant clergymen who advocated peace, civil rights, or social reform. His greatest support came from the least educated Americans, who believed his slander of even the mildest liberals as "treasonous agents of Moscow." A Gallup poll showed a majority of Americans supporting his crusade.

Professor Owen Lattimore, of Johns Hopkins University, was named by McCarthy as America's "top Russian agent," responsible for withdrawal of support from Chiang Kai-shek and so "turning over China to the Reds." This interpretation was peddled by the China Lobby—heavily financed by millionaire Alfred C. Kohlberg, an importer who had made a fortune out of Nationalist China—which wanted to influence American financial and military aid for Chiang. The China Lobby also worked through Joseph P. Kamp's Constitutional Educational League, which had been named in the mass sedition indictments of 1942 and 1943.

McCarthy made his accusation against Lattimore on the floor of the Senate, where he could not be sued for libel. He produced another former Communist turned informer, Louis Budenz, who gave hearsay testimony (inadmissible in any court of law) that he had been told by other Communists that Lattimore was a party member. Under later questioning, Budenz admitted having previously discussed Lattimore with Alfred Kohlberg.

McCarthy refused to allow Lattimore's lawyers to introduce in evidence an affidavit from Bella V. Dodd, a former leading Communist expelled from the party, that she had never once heard Lattimore's name mentioned. A Senate Foreign Relations subcommittee investigated and cleared Lattimore.

"We find no evidence to support the charge that Owen Lattimore is the 'top Russian spy' or, for that matter, any sort of spy," the report said; adding, "The Lattimore case affords an opportunity to reaffirm this nation's determination to protect its citizens when they . . . express freely their honest views and convictions."

In his book, *Ordeal by Slander,* Lattimore declared,

> The witch-hunting of which McCarthy is a part is recruited from ex-Communists and pro-Fascists, America Firsters, anti-Semites, Coughlinites and similar fringe fanatics of the political underworld. It was groups like these that Hitler used to run interference for him, causing the confusion and dismay that he and his real backers, the big-time reactionaries, needed in order to take over the state.

That McCarthy was a demagogue did not change the fact that some Americans had, or were still, engaged in treason for the Soviet Union. But these individuals were more likely to be under the professional observation of F.B.I. operatives than McCarthy's headline-hunters. J. Edgar Hoover noted that the genuine traitors were usually only a handful of party members, carefully and secretly selected by Moscow. Some had been compelled to spy because of threats to relatives in Russia; most served the Soviet Union for ideological reasons.

All of Moscow's American agents were made to sign incriminating papers and reports. "If the initial ideological enthusiasm wears off, as it probably will," Hoover explained, "the agent is trapped . . . he cannot break away."

Soviet spy Colonel Rudolph Abel operated for over seven years as chief of an espionage ring before he was caught. Typical of his American contacts were Manhattan teacher Morris Cohen and his Polish wife, Lola. Seven forged passports under a variety of names took them to different countries as Soviet agents. A C.I.A. tip to Scotland Yard brought about their arrest in England under the name of Kroger. Their suburban house was found full of espionage gadgets, a high-frequency transmitter, and micro-dot equipment to transmit British naval data. Each received twenty years in prison.

In March, 1950, a former Justice Department employee, Judith Coplon, and her sweetheart, Valentin Gubichev, a Soviet consular official, were indicted for conspiracy and attempted espionage. She was found guilty of copying F.B.I. reports on espionage and turning them over to Gubichev. He was expelled; Miss Coplon's conviction was set aside because of the illegal use of wiretapping evidence against her.

One of the most sensational series of espionage cases developed out of the arrest in Britain of physicist Klaus Fuchs, a German refugee who supplied information about American and British nuclear weapons to the Soviet Union. His data helped Moscow produce their own A-bomb some months earlier than they would have developed it on their own.

Ordered to the United States with other British physicists to work with American scientists during the war, he had relayed atomic data to Moscow through Harry Gold, a naturalized American of Russian parentage. Returning to England after the war, Fuchs continued to turn over atomic data to Russian agents but now accepted payment from them. In 1949, he was arrested by British security agents, tried, and sentenced to fourteen years in prison.

His confession implicated Harry Gold, who had been serving the Soviet Union as an industrial spy in America for fifteen years. Gold was a spy not because he was a Communist but primarily because he enjoyed espionage and liked inventing romantic lies about himself. He confessed his treason to the F.B.I. and promptly sought to win a lighter sentence by turning Government witness against others he named.

Chief figures of the spy ring, Gold said, were Ethel and Julius Rosenberg, a radical New York couple. Ethel's young brother, David Greenglass, was employed as a machinist in the atom-bomb project at Los Alamos, New Mexico. Gold alleged that Greenglass had been persuaded by the Rosenbergs to turn over A-bomb secrets to a spy courier who would be sent to him by a Soviet consular clerk. Gold was the courier.

Greenglass and the Rosenbergs were arrested by the F.B.I. Turning state's witness, Greenglass testified against his sister and her husband. Largely on his testimony and Gold's, the Rosenbergs were found guilty and sentenced to be electrocuted.

"I consider your crime," Judge Irving Kaufman told them, "worse than murder. . . . I believe your conduct in putting into the hands of the Russians the A-bomb . . . has already caused, in my opinion, the Communist aggression in Korea, with the resulting casualties exceeding fifty thousand and who knows but that millions more of innocent people may pay the price of your treason."

The case created a storm of controversy among millions who considered the Rosenbergs innocent. Some atomic scientists stated that the American public had been misled into believing in atomic "secrets," whereas the scientists of any major power could build an A-bomb exactly as the American physicists had done without any outside help.

Liberals worried that the Rosenbergs had been victims of a frame-up because of their radicalism in a Cold War climate of fear and hysteria. Doubts were raised over the testimony of Gold, who was a self-confessed imaginative liar, even under oath. Some critics were convinced that he had offered perjured evidence, full of holes and contradictions, in return for a promise of leniency in his own prosecution.

David Greenglass was also suspected of having been coached in the story he told, sacrificing his sister and her husband in a desperate attempt to save his own skin and spare his wife from prosecution. Throughout the trial the Rosenbergs steadfastly maintained their innocence, despite clear hints by the prosecution that they could avoid the death penalty by admitting guilt.

"Free the Rosenbergs" committees formed in London, Paris, Rome, Vienna, Copenhagen, and other cities. Appeals for clemency flooded into the White House from all over the world, including the Vatican. Even those who believed the Rosenbergs guilty felt that the death penalty had been too severe. But President Eisenhower refused to halt the execution.

As the hour of electrocution drew near, crowds gathered in dozens of major cities around the world to hold public prayer vigils for the Rosenbergs. In Paris, the American embassy, fearful of huge crowds gathering in the Place de la Concorde, called for protection. The embassy was surrounded by French troops armed with machine-guns and tear-gas.

The Rosenbergs died at Sing Sing on June 19, 1953, protesting their innocence to the last. Several subsequent investigations reached the conclusion that their guilt had not been proved; but that guilty or innocent, they had died as victims of political persecution.

Joseph P. Morray, visiting professor of law at Berkeley, raised some thoughtful questions: "What is the reason for our fury against Hiss, the Rosenbergs, Fuchs . . . ? Is it because they have refused to share with us a hatred for the Soviet Union? These people did wrong in violating the laws of their states. But the laws themselves and we who support and enforce them are not blameless. . . . We ought therefore to enforce them reluctantly and seek to avoid punishing acts done in good conscience."

When one of those laws, the Smith Act of 1946, was challenged in *Dennis et al. v. United States,* the Supreme Court upheld the act in 1951. Justice Hugo Black dissented, stating that the Smith Act violated the First Amendment. He called for a return to Justice Holmes's "clear and present danger" doctrine before advocacy of revolution could be punished.

Justice William O. Douglas agreed, finding that the teaching of "Marxist-Leninist doctrine" was not necessarily "conspiracy to overthrow" the government. Justice Robert Jackson also suggested that Communists represented little threat to any stable government: "The Communist recognizes that an established government in control of modern technology cannot be overthrown by force until it is about ready to fall of its own weight."

Nevada Senator Pat McCarran, chairman of the Senate Judiciary Committee, originated much of the "antitreason" legislation. In September, 1950, his McCarran Act required the registration of Communist and "Communist-front" organizations and the internment of Communists during a "national emergency" in six concentration camps with a capacity of 100,000 persons.

President Truman vetoed the bill, declaring: "The application of the registration requirements to so-called Communist-front organizations can be the greatest danger to freedom of speech, press and assembly since the Alien and Sedition laws of 1789." The bill was passed over his veto.

"It is enough to make Jefferson and Madison and Lincoln rise from their graves," declared the Pulitzer Prize–winning St. Louis *Post Dispatch.* Added the *Christian Century,* "Jefferson would have gone to jail."

In June, 1952, the McCarran-Walter Act changed U.S. immigration laws to screen out "subversives" and provide for deportation of immigrants and naturalized citizens for Communist and "Communist-front" affiliations.

McCarran, like other congressmen on the far Right, found no subversion among Fascists or pro-Fascists. After a visit to Franco Spain, he urged American loans to the dictator as a fine "anti-Communist" and ruler of "a civilized Christian nation." McCarran also urged that Jewish displaced persons be barred from the United States. "On the basis of my investigation," he claimed, the United States was admitting "persons who will not become good citizens and who will become ready recruits in subversive organizations."

The Anti-Defamation League accused him of "essential hostility toward Jews." Father Joseph L. Lamb, director of Social Service of the Rhode Island Diocese, said of the McCarran-Walter Act, "I am quite shocked and surprised in seeing Hitler's principles retained in our immigration legislation."

In 1954, an extension of the McCarran Act, the Communist Control Act, was introduced in the House. It required any person or organization cooperating with any Communist goals to register under the McCarran Act. The *Wall Street Journal* observed, "For all we know, the Communist party may be against juvenile delinquency. So is this newspaper."

But the bill passed, along with two more restrictive measures that year, the Espionage and Sabotage Act and the Immunity Act. Senator McCarthy, whose persistent and shrill Red-hunts continued to set the emotional climate for "national security" legislation, boasted, "There won't be enough cells in federal prisons when I get through!"

To McCarthy, almost every intellectual, every liberal, every Democrat, was an actual or potential traitor. He used his growing power to create panic and confusion in the Government itself, calling upon its two million employees to inform on each other and on department heads if they had any information about suspected Communist beliefs or tendencies.

During 1953 and 1954 McCarthy held a long series of hearings at which irresponsible attacks were made on the loyalty of respected Americans. President Eisenhower, increasingly outraged, began speaking out against McCarthy's squads of "book-burners," unfair conduct at the hearings, and attempts to saddle "thought control" on the American people.

McCarthy finally went too far when he staged televised hearings attacking the U.S. Army for concealing and protecting subversion. Forcing Army Secretary Robert T. Stevens and Brigadier General Ralph Zwicker to testify, McCarthy insulted Zwicker, telling him contemptuously he was not fit to wear the uniform. The American people, a majority of whom had until then supported McCarthy, were shocked as the TV cameras exposed him as an arrogant bully who bluffed, lied, distorted, sneered, and used outrageously unfair tactics.

The reaction was swift. Stunned Americans, ashamed of having thought of McCarthy as a hero, turned their backs on him. McCarthy was bewildered. He could not understand that he had made a serious tactical blunder in letting the public see him in action as he really was instead of letting them read glorifications of him in the right-wing press.

Republican Senator Ralph Flanders, of Vermont, comparing McCarthy to Hitler, introduced a resolution of censure against him, declaring, "Were the junior senator from Wisconsin in the pay of the Communists, he could not have done a better job for them." After an investigative committee reported, the Senate formally voted condemnation of McCarthy by a vote of 67 to 22.

His power broken at last and his dreams of becoming an American fuehrer in the White House destroyed, McCarthy rapidly slipped into oblivion and died soon afterward.

McCarthyism had been dealt a crushing blow—but not a fatal one. The far Right had other strings to its bow.

15

VIETNAM:
THE PRICE OF DISSENT

On the Atomic Energy Commission, one of the "security chiefs" in charge of evaluating the loyalty of atomic scientists such as Harold Urey, Leo Szilard, and J. Robert Oppenheimer was Medford Evans, who had written an article called, "Why I Am Anti-Intellectual." Evans later became Birch Society Coordinator for Texas and an adviser to General Edwin Walker, who was relieved of his command for subverting his troops.

Perhaps one of the most celebrated victims of McCarthyism was J. Robert Oppenheimer, a nuclear physicist internationally acclaimed for his brilliance. In 1936 he had found himself deeply disturbed by current events. His students were finding it difficult to get suitable jobs because of the Depression. His Jewish relatives in Germany were being threatened by the Nazis. Germany and Italy were sending troops, planes, and tanks to help Franco overthrow democracy in Spain.

Tens of thousands of American intellectuals were becoming political activists. Among those who joined the Communist party were Oppenheimer's wife, brother, and sister-in-law. He, however, like the great majority of liberal intellectuals, simply joined the anti-Fascist movement. President Eisenhower later described him as politically naïve but certified that he had not been involved in any subversive movement.

The Hitler-Stalin Pact of 1939 disillusioned the Oppenheimers. He was further dismayed by Stalin's purge of three Russian physicists he respected. His wife dropped out of the Communist party, and he left the anti-Fascist United Front.

After Pearl Harbor Oppenheimer did such valuable work for the Government defense effort that he was asked to take charge of building an American atomic bomb. He revealed his former membership in left-wing groups but was assured that this would not deny him security clearance for the project.

Gathering about him the top physicists in America, Oppenheimer became the guiding genius of the stupendous secret research and development project at Los Alamos. He saw no reason to discontinue seeing close personal friends who had been, or still were, Communists or leftists; the Soviet Union was now America's war ally and "respectable."

Through George Eltenton, British chemical engineer, Soviet scientists suggested to Oppenheimer that informal exchanges of atomic information could help the Allied war effort against Germany. Upset by this unofficial approach, Oppenheimer warned Colonel John Lansdale, project-security officer at Los Alamos, that Eltenton might bear watching. However, he concealed the name of the friend who had conveyed Eltenton's message to him, not wanting to get him in trouble.

Oppenheimer was one of the scientists who recommended dropping the A-bomb on Japan to end the war quickly. President Truman awarded him the Medal of Merit, declaring, "More than any other one man, Oppenheimer is to be credited with the achievement of the atomic bomb." He cited the scientist's "outstanding service to the War Department . . . and his unswerving devotion to duty." Oppenheimer was appointed adviser to the U.N. Atomic Energy Committee Scientific Panel as well as to the U.S. Atomic Energy Commission.

But he became increasingly uneasy about leaving atomic weapons in the hands of the generals and urged that they be put under civilian control. He also pleaded for international control of the weapons to prevent a terrible nuclear-arms race. These views infuriated powerful figures in the State Department and the Pentagon, coming as they did in the midst of the deepening Cold War. Rumors began to circulate that Oppenheimer was secretly sympathetic to the Russians.

Eminent Americans such as Dr. James Conant and Bernard Baruch and many indignant nuclear physicists rushed to his defense, branding the rumors absurd. Oppenheimer persisted in advocating international cooperation on atomic energy so that it might be used for the peaceful benefit of all mankind. There were no such things as "atomic secrets," he warned; any major nation's physicists could develop an A-bomb. In August, 1949, Americans were stunned when the Soviet Union exploded theirs.

The Pentagon demanded that American scientists quickly press ahead and develop a super-bomb—the H-bomb—which Dr. Edward Teller assured the generals could be made. Oppenheimer and the General Advisory Committee to the Atomic Energy Commission warned that it could only lead to a deadly arms-race that might end in the destruction of the world.

But Cold War hysteria prevailed; the H-bomb was built and exploded in November, 1952. Less than two years later Russia had its own hydrogen bomb, and the atomic race skyrocketed as each side kept perfecting delivery systems.

McCarthyism led to a challenge of Oppenheimer's right to access to American atomic secrets. "More probably than not," declared his accuser, William L. Borden, a former minor official, "he has acted . . . [as] an espionage agent." At an Atomic Energy Commission hearing, Oppenheimer's security clearance was revoked, and he was denied access to restricted atomic data as a "security risk." It was tantamount to a civilian court-martial branding him guilty of disloyalty.

Not until December, 1963, when Cold War hysteria had abated, did the Atomic Energy Commission seek to apologize by presenting Oppenheimer with the highest honor it could bestow —the Enrico Fermi Award. President Lyndon B. Johnson made the presentation at the White House. When Oppenheimer died three years later, representatives of twenty-five nations of the world halted an international conference on nuclear arms control to pay tribute to the man his country had labeled a "security risk."

In 1955, Attorney General Howard J. McGrath, speaking to the American Bar Association, said, "We appear to be going through a period of public hysteria in which many varieties of self-appointed policemen, and alleged guardians of Americanism, would have us fight subversion by proscribing an orthodoxy of opinion, and stigmatizing as disloyal all who disagree with them."

Robert Williams, a Negro ex-Marine, was so angry at the treatment of blacks in America that he wrote to President Eisenhower in 1955, expressing his desire to renounce his citizenship. Four years later, as head of the Monroe, North Carolina, N.A.A.C.P., he began to arm its members, insisting, "Negroes . . . must henceforth meet violence with violence." Suspended by the N.A.A.C.P., he went to Cuba and returned a confirmed "Fidelista."

In 1961 he was charged with kidnapping and holding a white couple as hostages until police rescued them. Fleeing to Cuba, Williams was given asylum as a political refugee. He told American blacks over Radio Havana, "Not only does freedom require the will to die, but it also requires the will to kill. . . . Let us meet violence with violence."

He formed an organization called RAM—Revolutionary Action Movement, Black Liberation Front of the U.S.A.— which helped train American Negroes in Cuba in guerrilla warfare and sabotage. When Cuban Communists cooled toward Williams, he left in the spring of 1966 for Red China.

Two RAM members were subsequently arrested in New York for conspiring to murder moderate black leaders Roy Wilkins and Whitney Young; fifteen others were arrested for violating the New York State criminal-anarchy law. In Philadelphia RAM members were arrested for plotting a riot at which the lunches of policemen sent to fight would be poisoned.

In December, 1967, Williams, now in Africa, declared that he planned to return home to face charges against him, clear himself, and run as a black-power candidate for President. Four months later the Malcolm X Society held a convention in Detroit, signing a declaration of independence calling for a separate Negro nation in the South. Robert Williams was elected President and H. Rap Brown Minister of Defense.

When Williams sought to return home in 1969, Trans World Airlines refused to let him board its plane in London, claiming "such transportation would or might be inimical to the safety of the flight." Upon protest by the Civil Liberties Union, T.W.A. finally flew him to the United States as the sole passenger of a plane that normally carried 130 passengers.

In the late 1950s the Supreme Court began administering some stinging rebuffs to McCarthyism. *Pennsylvania v. Nelson* (1956) held the state's antisubversive legislation unconstitutional for usurping the federal right to determine and suppress subversion. *Watkins v. U.S.* (1957) set aside the contempt conviction of a labor-union official for refusing to name other Communist-party members he had known in earlier years.

Yates v. U.S. (1957) put a stop to over one hundred indict-

ments and convictions under the Smith Act since the imprisonment of the Communist-party leaders. The Court held that no one
could be charged under the Smith Act if he simply advocated or
taught forcible overthrow of the government as an abstract
principle, with no proven effort to incite a specific act.

The Court also sought to stop discrimination against Americans who considered compulsory loyalty oaths degrading and
unconstitutional. In *First Unitarian Church v. Los Angeles*
(1958) the Court ordered restoration of tax-exemption rights
for Unitarian church property, which had been denied the Uni-
tarians for refusing to take oaths swearing they did not advocate
violent overthrow of the Government or support of any foreign
government. The Court found that they had been denied their
rights under the Fourteenth Amendment.

Such decisions, following the historic 1954 decision of the
Court, *Brown v. Board of Education of Topeka,* which held
school segregation to be illegal, infuriated the extreme Right in
America. The principal targets of their wrath were Supreme
Court Chief Justice Earl Warren and Justice William O. Douglas.

The Birch Society was formed in Indianapolis in December,
1958, by Joseph Welch, a retired candy manufacturer. Dedicated to the principles of McCarthyism, the Birchites revived the
Christian Front spirit of the Coughlinites, attracting the cooperation of other far-Right extremist groups.

Founder Joseph Welch attacked democracy as "merely a de-
ceptive phrase, a weapon of demagoguery, and a perennial
fraud." He denounced President Eisenhower as "a dedicated,
conscious agent of the Communist conspiracy," along with other
such "Red" agents as Milton Eisenhower, John Foster Dulles,
and General George Marshall. President Roosevelt had been
guilty of "plain unadulterated treason." And Justice Warren had
to be impeached for "converting this republic into a democracy."

Thomas Anderson of the Birch Society National Council proposed, "Why not hold some treason trials? The perfect site for

treason trials would be Hyde Park." Those who should be put on
trial at Roosevelt's homesite, he hinted, included Presidents
Truman, Eisenhower, and Kennedy, along with their respective
Secretaries of State.

In July, 1961, the *Birch Society Bulletin* estimated that there
were "300,000 to 500,000 Communists in the United States"
and "not more than a million allies, dupes and sympathizers."
Liberals were included in the society's private lists of "subversives" because they were "trying to change the economic and
political structure of the country so that it could be comfortably
merged with Soviet Russia."

Another far-Right voice warning of a Red takeover was that of
the Reverend Billy James Hargis, who conducted a million-
dollar Christian Crusade Against Communism from Tulsa,
Oklahoma. Hargis denounced the U.N. as "that traitorous outfit in New York City" and named as the "betrayers" of America
"Time magazine, National Council of Churches hierarchy,
Washington *Post,* N.A.A.C.P., and all other liberals and interna-
tionalists."

Major General Edwin A. Walker, who was removed from his
command for propagandizing his troops with Birchite materials,
appeared before Congress to assail many distinguished public
figures as "soft on Communism" and charge that a mysterious
"control apparatus" linked to Secretary of State Dean Rusk was
working on behalf of the Soviet Union.

These charges raised questions of his sanity and caused even
ultra-conservative William F. Buckley, Jr., to admit, "The verdict is that General Walker be consigned to history's ashcan, and
that henceforth his name call forth the roars of contempt and
ridicule." Walker incited a racist mob at the University of Mississippi against permitting the registration of its first Negro,
James Meredith. Arrested, he was charged with inciting rebellion and insurrection, and the Government ordered him to be
given a psychiatric examination.

Walker later turned up to lead a turbulent demonstration in Dallas against the United Nations; next day a screaming mob of his followers physically attacked Adlai Stevenson when he attempted to speak in that city. They also distributed "Wanted" posters with President John F. Kennedy's face and the headline: "WANTED FOR TREASON against the United States." Four weeks later the President was assassinated in Dallas.

Birch Society member Robert Bolivar DePugh founded a group called The Minutemen, with units in forty states and all major cities. His troops had hidden field pieces, machine guns, and other weapons and held "Guerrilla Warfare Seminars" regularly as a "patriotic duty."

DePugh justified his private army by citing HUAC's 1960 report stating that since Communist tactics were designed to render conventional military forces ineffective, the American people might have to rely on other forces for defense against armed subversion. Former Governor Pat Brown warned that there were twenty-four hundred of DePugh's "armed rightists" in California alone.

In 1968, HUAC issued a report called *Guerrilla Warfare Advocates in the United States*. It listed dozens of Communist, black-nationalist, and other left-wing groups but made not one mention of The Minutemen or any of the other innumerable private far-Right guerrilla armies in the nation.

Nazi leader Hermann Goering once explained how to saddle a dictatorship on a country: "Tell the people they are threatened. Throw the pacifists in jail for threatening the security of the nation. It's as simple as that and it works in any country."

Throughout the decade of the sixties and into the seventies, the burning question of treason centered around the highly controversial Vietnam war, perhaps the most unpopular war in all American history. It was an undeclared war, so that technically the statute of treason could not be applied.

But the issue was nevertheless one of treason versus patriotism. Those who supported the Government insisted that it was the duty of all Americans to support the war ("My country, right or wrong"). Those who opposed the war as immoral, unjust, and a tragic blunder declared that the true course of patriotism lay in opposing the war in every way possible, to get America out of its unfortunate involvement in Asia.

Anti-Vietnam demonstrations involved burning draft cards, burning the American flag, sitting-in at induction centers, lying down in front of troop trains, breaking into draft centers and burning files, protesting against ROTC and Defense Department research projects at the nation's universities.

Taking part in antiwar demonstrations were ministers, priests, rabbis, doctors, professors, scientists, Nobel Prize–winners, and such celebrated national figures as Dr. Martin Luther King, Jr. A leader of the anti-Vietnam movement emerged in Senator Eugene McCarthy, of Minnesota, who challenged President Johnson's renomination in the election campaign of 1968. He scored upsetting successes in the primaries, causing Johnson to decide against running for reelection.

In November, 1965, Republican Senator Thomas Kuchel excoriated "the vicious, venomous and vile leaders of this infamous movement who attempt to influence young people of this country to evade the draft by fraud and chicanery." He demanded an investigation by the Justice Department, insisting, "What has gone on sows the seeds of treason!"

HUAC hearings on antiwar demonstrations at Berkeley spotlighted student publications that advocated sabotage against the Vietnam war as "the only remaining route to peace." *Open Process* urged:

Break war-related laws: draft, security, federal trespassing. Damage war equipment. Join with your fellow workers in strikes, slowdowns, and "botching the job" in key war in-

dustries. . . . Publish state secrets you have access to.
. . . People have a right to know what "their" government
is up to.

Most antiwar protesters, however, were nonviolent, limiting
their protests to demonstrations and symbolic acts of civil disobedience in the tradition of Thoreau and Gandhi. They demanded an end to the bombing of North Vietnam; of the use of
napalm bombs against peasant women and children; of the
burning of "suspected" villages; of the torture of captured Viet
Cong soldiers; of the massacre of women and children in territory controlled by the Viet Cong.

In opposing the Vietnam war for humanitarian reasons, they
insisted, they were simply living up to the principles established
by the United States Government at the Nuremberg Trials in
condemning "crimes against humanity." The dissenters cited
world condemnation of the United States role in Vietnam, pointing out the irony of an American government, born in revolution, seeking to put down a patriotic revolution against the
unpopular dictatorship of the South Vietnam regime.

In May, 1967, Representative L. Mendel Rivers, chairman of
the House Armed Services Committee, demanded prosecution of
Americans counseling, aiding, and abetting avoidance of the
draft. Assistant Attorney General Fred M. Vinson, Jr., replied
that the First Amendment barred such prosecutions.

"Let's forget about the First Amendment!" snapped Representative Herbert, of Louisiana. In October, antiwar demonstrations at the Pentagon angered General Lewis B. Hershey,
Selective Service Director, who ordered the nation's draft boards
to call up immediately any registrant who interfered with the
draft or was involved in antiwar demonstrations.

The Justice Department informed Hershey that punitive re-
classification was illegal and unconstitutional and that no regis-

trant could be punished for protesting against the war or the draft. Hershey refused to rescind his order, stating that it had been authorized by the White House. But local draft boards soon learned to disregard it whenever they were challenged by the Civil Liberties Union, which took such cases up to the Supreme Court and won them.

The Johnson Administration felt that it had to do something to stop the mounting draft resistance. In January, 1968, Dr. Benjamin Spock, the renowned baby doctor, the Reverend William Sloane Coffin, of Yale, and three colleagues were indicted, charged with conspiracy to "counsel, aid, and abet" violations of the draft law.

The defendants argued that they had been within their rights of freedom of speech and assembly. As for "conspiracy," it was pointed out that all the acts complained of by the Government were done openly in front of TV cameras, including their issue of a "Call to Resist Illegitimate Authority." The trial was obviously a political one, they charged, meant to intimidate other leaders of the antiwar movement.

The Boston trial judge went out of his way to influence the jury by giving them ten guidelines to use in deciding the guilt of the accused. The jury freed one defendant, found the other four guilty. Each received a two-year jail sentence.

But the First U.S. Circuit Court of Appeals in Boston soon overturned the conviction, finding that the lower-court judge's guidelines to the jury had been prejudicial. The defendants had also been right in stating that "vigorous criticism of the draft and of the Vietnam war is . . . protected by the First Amendment, even though its effect is to interfere with the war effort." Dr. Spock and one defendant were freed; charges against Dr. Coffin and another were later dropped.

"It seems to me absolutely tragic," Dr. Spock declared after his release, "that young Americans will continue to die in Vietnam . . . and that young men have been imprisoned for being opposed to it and doing as their consciences dictated."

Another trial of anti-Establishment dissenters was soon to shake and confuse Americans even more.

16

"A POLICE RIOT"

In the summer of 1967 President Johnson reactivated the Subversive Activities Control Board, which had performed no functions for the past eighteen months. But two years later a unanimous Court of Appeals decision invalidated the board as unconstitutional, along with the board's required registration of alleged Communists.

Turbulence marked the election year of 1968. There were civil disorders, ghetto riots, antiwar and antidraft protests, student revolts, a poor people's march on Washington, and the shocking assassinations of Martin Luther King, Jr., and Robert Kennedy.

An alarmed Congress saw these chaotic developments as signs of a left-wing conpiracy, instead of as symptoms of widespread frustration and anger over the Administration's persistence in waging the Vietnam war while neglecting the urgent problems of the black, the poor, and the young at home.

After a race riot sparked by black militant H. Rap Brown, Congress added an antiriot clause to the Civil Rights Act of

1968, making it a crime to cross state lines with the intention of provoking a riot. The law did not intimidate the nation's antiwar dissenters into giving up their plan for a confrontation with the Administration at the Democratic National Convention scheduled for Chicago in late August.

Their intention was to influence the delegates, by demonstrations outside the convention hall, to reject the Administration's policies and deny the Presidential nomination to Vice President Hubert Humphrey. Their choice was Senator Eugene McCarthy, whose candidacy had become the symbol of the antiwar movement. His young, idealistic supporters were joined by more radical anti-Establishment hippies and yippies.

Mayor Richard J. Daley, of Chicago, denied the demonstrators places to hold rallies or demonstrations and turned the convention hall into an armed fortress. Anti-Administration Democratic delegates, as well as members of the press, were roughly handled by the Chicago police. Daley augmented the police force with National Guardsmen and Army troops, insisting that they were needed to preserve law and order in the face of threatened violence.

There were bloody clashes between police and demonstrators. Young people were attacked and beaten up, subjected to teargas and Mace, and dragged into police vans. TV cameramen filming some of these scenes were also attacked by police. Indignant delegates at the convention angrily denounced Mayor Daley for using "Gestapo tactics."

Daley defended the police by insisting that they had been provoked by insults and filth hurled by some of the demonstrators, although he admitted that "some" police might have "overreacted" to the provocation. Ironically, millions of Americans who were shocked at the scenes of violence in Chicago they saw on TV were not indignant at the clubbing of McCarthy's young supporters but at the TV networks for showing it.

An impartial commission was appointed by the President to investigate the Chicago riots. The resultant Walker Report concluded, "To read dispassionately the hundreds of statements describing at first hand the events of Sunday and Monday nights is to become convinced of what can only be called a police riot."

The New York Times blamed the Daley regime for causing the disorders in the first place by denying the right of assembly to protesting groups and for using excessive and indiscriminate force to stifle the dissent that was obviously doing serious political damage to the Democratic party.

Eight young "New Left" leaders of the demonstrators were indicted in Chicago for conspiracy to cross state lines to incite a riot. No Chicago police were indicted for assaulting demonstrators and spectators. As the Walker Report noted, "There has been no public condemnation of these violators of sound police procedures and common decency by either their commanding officers or city officials."

HUAC held hearings on the "Subversive Involvement in Disruption of 1968 Democratic Party National Convention," seeking to prove that the young dissenters under indictment had conspired to cause the trouble in Chicago and disrupt the convention. Thomas Hayden, former president of the Students for a Democratic Society (S.D.S.), was interrogated by HUAC counsel Frank Conley.

Hayden accused HUAC of trying to paint the antiwar movement "as somehow being an aggressive, violent movement. It is a case of the criminal calling the victim the criminal." He admitted having gone to North Vietnam to meet with Communist officials, stating that he wanted "to try to understand the outlook on peace and war that the other side held."

He added, "My Government, which I don't think represents me, is wrong in Vietnam." Accused of trying to destroy the present American democratic system, he replied, "That is a joke.

. . . I don't believe the present American democratic system exists. . . . You have destroyed [it] by the existence of a committee of this kind."

Asked whether he believed that the young revolutionary movement he represented really expected to succeed, he brought laughter by replying dryly, "Well, I think we will at least outlive you." He added calmly, "Probably much of our time will be spent in penitentiaries."

Hayden considered support of the Vietnam war to be "patriotic in the worst sense." He said, "I think the symbols of patriotism have been stolen by the Right, and they have to be regained by those people who are working to make freedom and peace in this country consistent with American interests."

The Chicago Eight were put on trial in that city before Judge Julius Hoffman. It was a political trial that brought the Justice Department under Attorney General John Mitchell into stark confrontation with the New Left. The proceedings were kept in an uproar from start to finish by clashes between the unruly defendants and the prickly judge.

When one defendant, black militant Bobby Seale, refused to be silenced, Judge Hoffman ordered him bound to his seat and gagged. The spectacle was so repellent to ideas of American justice that the judge sentenced him instead to four years in jail for contempt of court and remanded him for separate trial at a later date.

For five months the other seven defendants continued to disrupt the trial. They challenged Judge Hoffman as a biased judge who granted every motion of the prosecution and denied every motion of the defense. When former Attorney General Ramsey Clark and Rev. Ralph David Abernathy, Martin Luther King's successor, sought to testify in their behalf, Judge Hoffman refused to allow them to be heard.

The defendants made no secret of their contempt for the

brand of justice dispensed in Chicago. While the jury was out deliberating on a verdict, Judge Hoffman sentenced all the defendants and their attorney, William Kunstler, to a total of over fifteen years in jail on 160 separate counts of contempt.

After four days of deliberation, the jury returned a verdict acquitting two defendants and finding the other five innocent of conspiracy but guilty of crossing state lines with the intention of inciting to riot. Three of the jurors considered the law unconstitutional but were persuaded to agree on a compromise verdict so that the law could be tested by a Supreme Court review of the case on appeal.

Judge Hoffman sentenced each of the convicted five defendants to the maximum term of five years, with a five-thousand-dollar fine plus court costs. At first he tried to keep them in jail on exorbitant bail, pending appeal, as men "too dangerous" to be at large, but he was finally compelled to free them on lower bail on condition they stay out of further trouble.

The trial shook the judicial system of the United States, worrying the bar associations. The Seven had entered Judge Hoffman's courtroom convinced that the Establishment they opposed would not give them a fair trial. Feeling they owed it no respect, they had yelled, hooted, laughed, and clowned all through the proceedings.

Many bar associations felt that the Government should never have put on what was obviously a political trial. While condemning the actions of the defendants in turning the courtroom into a propaganda platform, they deplored equally the violations of fair judicial practice by the presiding judge.

Professor Larry Nachman, a political scientist at the City College of New York, observed in *The Nation:*

> The weight, authority, and legitimacy of the United States Government was put behind Daley and the Chicago police.

This action instantly distorted history. Once the trial began, one could retain one's original view of the Chicago violence only at the cost of raising some deep and ugly questions about the nature of the United States Government that was prosecuting the case. . . . The primary wrong in the trial was not the partiality, unfairness and vindictiveness of the judge but his willingness to permit the Government to use a federal court to legitimatize violence against its opponents.

As the trial ended, the chief question was whether the Court of Appeals would overturn Judge Hoffman's sentences on the basis of judicial errors. If it did not, the case would go to the U.S. Supreme Court, which would then decide whether the federal law against crossing a state line with intent to create a riot was a violation of the First Amendment.

Meanwhile, a 1970 Supreme Court decision upheld the right of judges to use whatever means of restraint were necessary to maintain decorum in the courtroom, even to banning a defendant from attending his own trial, if necessary.

The violence in Chicago seemed to signal the end of an era of political confrontation and the beginning of revolutionary opposition to the Government. Millions of youthful dissenters were disillusioned with their inability to "change things around" by working within the political system.

"We're convinced now," one militant said, "the Establishment is deaf to any argument except an exploding bank."

Serious clashes began taking place between the outspoken revolutionary Black Panthers and the police departments of various cities. Police raids on Panther headquarters resulted in shoot-outs during which both Panthers and police were killed and wounded. Many Panther headquarters proved to be heavily stocked with weapons, which the Panthers insisted were solely for self-defense. They saw the raids as part of a plan by Attorney General Mitchell to wipe out the black-militant movement. The Justice Department denied it.

Police quoted Max Stanford, of the Black Panther party, at a 1966 rally, according to an Associated Press dispatch:

> Stanford took the podium. Flanked by members of the Black Panther group, he said "black men" must unite in overthrowing their white "oppressors," but must do it "like panthers—smiling, cunning, scientifically . . . striking by night and sparing no one." Stanford said the U.S. could be brought down with "a rag and some gasoline and a bottle" —the ingredients of a fire bomb.

If the Panthers were using fire bombs in race riots or against police cars, other bombs were the weapons of a militant faction of S.D.S. called The Weatherman. Giving up all hope of "reforming the system," The Weatherman took to the tactics of blowing up symbols of capitalism. On the West Coast a Bank of America building was destroyed by bombing, and in New York City the General Telephone and Electronics, General Motors, and IBM buildings were bombed. The bombers gave advance warning of their targets so that no persons would be hurt.

When Rennie Davis, one of the Chicago Seven, was asked how he felt about these bombings in a TV interview, he replied that the radicals had destroyed only a few "capitalist buildings," whereas the American Government had bombed and destroyed over a million men, women, and children in Vietnam and still had not stopped. Which, he demanded, was more violent?

He was answered by New York *Post* columnist James Wechsler, who pointed out that by the tactics of anarchy, the New Left would only provoke heavy repression in reprisal from the Government. Not only would New Leftists be crushed, but they would at the same time badly hurt the chances of persuading the American people to correct the injustices that were alienating the young, the black, the poor, and the liberal.

The big question for the seventies was whether the American Government could or would move swiftly enough to reform the system, as the New Deal had done in the crisis of the thirties.

The Bank of America bombing, cautioned University of California sociologists Richard Flacks and Milton Mankoff, "ought to warn this country's managers that they have just about exhausted the loyalty of the country's youth. . . . Once they have lost faith in legitimate authority and see normal channels blocked, the political newcomers express their rage in ways less tempered by questions of proper strategy and tactics."

They foresaw a rapid radicalization of middle-class youth unless the Government soon ended the war in Vietnam and solved America's desperate problems at home.

New York mayor John V. Lindsay also saw the problem as one of the nation's institutions failing the hungry, the poor, the black, and the young, creating anger among them. "I share that anger," he said. He did not, however, justify terrorism because of valid grievances. "It is cowardly," he declared, "and it is immoral. If you claim to believe the Vietnam war is immoral—if you understand why the burning of a village and the slaughter of civilians is an abhorrent act—then your job and my job is not to open up a new frontier for bloodshed, but to stop it everywhere, once and for all."

But Lindsay also warned of allowing the Government to use repression to crush dissent: "We have seen all too clearly that there are men—now in power in this country—who do not respect dissent, who cannot cope with turmoil, and who believe that the people of America are ready to support repression as long as it is done with a quiet voice and a business suit. And it is up to us to prove that they are wrong."

17

DISLOYALTY VERSUS DISSENT

Now it is time to try to answer some of the questions about disloyalty and dissent raised in the first chapter; or at least to recognize guidelines for an intelligent approach to the problems raised.

Does the Government have the right to use repressive measures to protect itself from overthrow? How far can it legally go—against whom, and under what circumstances?

Certainly every government in the world seeks to prevent its own overthrow from within or without. It claims the loyalty of its citizens in exchange for the rights and privileges they enjoy under its aegis. Trouble arises when a group of citizens feels that a law or action of the government is so unjust or bad that they, like Thoreau, must disobey it.

The Government has sought to punish them by legal prosecution, as in the cases of Debs, Spock, and the Chicago Seven, or to combat them with congressional or security-agency probes, as in the cases of Hiss, Oppenheimer, and the Hollywood Ten.

The needs of national security need to be weighed against the dangers of treating dissent as disloyalty. The loyalty probes of Oppenheimer and other scientists who disagreed with government policy in the fifties made many American scientists afraid to offer constructive criticism of the nation's military research. Some refused to attend important international scientific conferences for fear of being suspected of contact with Communist scientists. Others quit government service rather than curb their free scientific inquiry.

Another risk of cracking down hard on dissent is that the dissenters, like the Weathermen, of S.D.S., are driven underground, where they are far more dangerous to the Government. When the Johnson and Nixon Administrations took repressive measures against the protests led by S.D.S. against the Vietnam war, the organization split into nonviolent and violent (Weatherman) factions. The Weatherman then began to protest by bombing banks, business buildings, and police stations.

Americans alleged by the Government to be disloyal or treasonous may actually be so, like Benedict Arnold or William Dudley Pelley. But it must also be kept in mind that throughout American history the cry of treason has been raised as a political weapon to silence embarrassing questions about an administration's failures or shortcomings, as the John Adams Administration did against the Jeffersonians and the Lyndon Johnson Administration did against antiwar senators.

To prevent the political misuse of the treason charge, the Founding Fathers carefully defined the crime, and the proofs required, in Article III, Section 3, of the Constitution. Some Congresses, however, have evaded this restriction by punishing alleged treason under different names in such loosely drawn legislation as the McCarran, McCarran-Walter, Communist Control, and Smith Acts.

At the height of Cold War hysteria in the early fifties, Congress debated whether to outlaw the Communist party as subversive, in order to protect American security.

"If we outlaw the Communist party," said Representative Emanuel Celler, of New York, "there is no reason why if the Republicans are in control they could not outlaw the Democratic party. . . . You could say that any party that opposes high tariffs or believes in deficit spending is subversive."

In point of fact, Senator Joseph McCarthy had crusaded against the liberal record of the Democratic party as "twenty years of treason," and at the height of his power public-opinion polls showed that a majority of Americans supported him.

Unless we violate the Bill of Rights, we cannot single out any political group and declare it illegal, no matter how much we detest its policies. The rights of dissenters are what distinguish our democracy from Communist or Fascist dictatorships. We might also question the wisdom of harassing unpopular political minorities by either punitive legislation or police action.

France, England, Italy, the Scandinavian countries, and many others permit the Communist party and all other radical parties to operate openly in opposition to the Government. The result is that their dissent is peaceful and works for change within the political system.

But what about Fascist groups like the Christian Front, the Silver Shirts, and the Minutemen, who seek a right-wing dictatorship in the style of Hitler, Mussolini, and Franco?

Fascists have the same political rights under the Constitution as Communists or any other radicals. If they are guilty of treason, the Department of Justice has an obligation to bring such charges in court. If they are not guilty of treason, they are protected by the Bill of Rights.

It is true that both the far Right and the far Left are dedicated to undermining our democracy. The far Left has been urging violence and revolution as the only way to bring about needed change, insisting that the Government will neither listen to nor act upon grievances.

Abraham I. Pomerantz, who was deputy chief counsel of the

American legal staff at the Nazi trials in Nuremberg, explained
far-Right tactics:

> The approach, copied from the Nazis, works this way: The
> press and radio first lay down a terrific barrage against the
> Red Menace. Headlines without a shred of evidence shriek
> of atom bomb spies or plots to overthrow the government,
> of espionage, of high treason, and of other bloodcurdling
> crimes. We are now ready for the second stage: the pinning
> of the label "Red" indiscriminately on all opposition.

American security may be better protected from extremist
propaganda by open and searching discussion of the claims
made by the far Right and the far Left than by jailing the
propagandists. On June 14, 1953, President Eisenhower denounced Senator Joseph McCarthy's attempt to outlaw books
discussing communism in a speech at Dartmouth. "How will we
defeat communism," the President demanded, "unless we know
what it is, and what it teaches, and why does it have such an
appeal for men?"

Is it disloyal for Americans of foreign ancestry to maintain
cultural ties to the country of their fathers?

As a nation of immigrants, it would be surprising if Americans of Italian descent did not feel a kinship with Italian relatives, those of Irish descent with Irish relatives, those of German
descent with German relatives, those of Jewish descent with
Israeli relatives, those of Japanese descent with Japanese relatives. Their cultural heritage and sympathies have little to do
with their basic loyalty to America.

As we saw, the John Adams Administration directed harsh
alien and sedition laws against French immigrants during a time
of strained relations with France. American Catholic immigrants in the nineteenth century were often persecuted as traitors

because of their religious allegiance to Rome. Patriotic Nisei were put in World War II concentration camps simply because of their Japanese ancestry.

Reason and justice would suggest that in time of crisis, all Americans should be considered equally loyal, regardless of their cultural or blood ties to a hostile nation, until there is legal evidence to prove that they are not.

How can we determine the dividing line between dissent and disloyalty? There is perhaps no thornier question.

It is, first of all, important to distinguish between disloyalty to the nation and total opposition to the policies of a particular administration. The Jeffersonians were not traitors because they wholly opposed the anti-French war policies of the Adams Administration, although the Federalists insisted that this opposition was treason. Likewise, when the Jeffersonians took over the White House, the Federalists were not traitors for wholly opposing the anti-British war policies of the Jefferson Administration, although the Jeffersonians insisted that *their* opposition was now treason.

Perhaps all of us could agree that political opposition of any kind should never be regarded as treason, since today's Government policies may be proved to be wrong tomorrow and changed around completely. No better modern example can be cited than the Vietnam war. The Johnson Administration branded as traitors those who called it a mistake and demanded that American troops be withdrawn. The Nixon Administration agreed it was a mistake and reversed American policy by gradually withdrawing our forces from Vietnam.

Assuming that the Vietnam war and drafting troops for it was a mistake, was the American minority that opposed it justified in breaking the law to try to stop what they considered an illegal and immoral war? This question inevitably raises a deeper problem. Can a minority be allowed to decide which laws of a majority they will obey as just laws and which laws they will defy as unjust?

"Are laws to be enforced simply because they were made, or declared by any number of men to be good," Thoreau asked in opposing the Mexican War, "if they are *not* good?"

But the very meaning of democracy is that the laws of the majority must prevail. If each individual is free to obey only laws he likes, there is no rule of law but only anarchy. To *disagree* with any government law or policy, and agitate for its repeal, is every citizen's right. But he does not have the right to disobey a law unless he is willing to pay the prescribed penalty for his defiance.

On the other hand, many dissenters feel that it is wrong for the majority to force a minority to obey laws the minority considers unjust. During the fifties some scientists broke national security laws to share atomic knowledge with other scientists abroad in the interest of world peace.

"Where does a man's loyalty lie?" asked British biologist Michael Amrine in his book, *Treason*. "Is loyalty to the race larger than loyalty to the nation? . . . If I lie, I am false not only to you, but to myself, to my science, to my civilization, and, as I believe, false to the best interests of my country. . . . It is madness."

Deeply religious persons have also been prosecuted and jailed for activities opposing the draft, a war, or laws discriminating against blacks or the poor. Among them have been Quakers, priests, ministers, and rabbis convinced that they had no choice but to place their beliefs about God and a "higher morality" above the demands of the state.

Perhaps if such Americans must be arrested to uphold the authority of the law, their arrests should be made with a public acknowledgment that they are regrettable. Those willing to go to jail out of the convictions of their conscience also deserve, at least, to have their beliefs fully reported to the American people. If enough of us are convinced that they are right, we owe it to our own consciences to insist that Congress change the unjust law.

How should treason be judged and punished?

American justice requires that anyone accused of treason be presumed innocent until proved guilty in court after a fair trial on the basis of factual evidence. As we have seen, however, many Americans have been persecuted as "traitors" through the device of a one-sided congressional-committee hearing, with no opportunity to cross-examine witnesses against them. Condemned by hearsay evidence inadmissible in any court of law, they have also been smeared by such police-state principles as "guilt by association."

The need for such congressional inquisitions to protect American security is questionable, at best. Almost all real cases of treason, espionage, and sabotage have been uncovered, and successfully prosecuted, by the F.B.I. and the intelligence sections of the armed forces.

Any government has the right to protect itself against revolutionists who seek to overthrow it by violence. In view of our own history, however, one wonders if American revolutionists can be prosecuted for treason. Were the American revolutionists of 1776 traitors for conspiring to overthrow the legal British Government they were sworn to uphold? Were American southerners traitors in 1861 when they conspired to rebel against the Federal Government?

Many antisubversive laws have tried to make it a crime to teach, study, or predict revolution. In his Dartmouth speech President Eisenhower said, "We have got to fight it with something better, not try to conceal the thinking of our own people. They are part of America. And even if they think ideas that are contrary to ours, their right to say them, their right to record them, and their right to have them at places where they are accessible to others is unquestioned, or it isn't America."

Few Americans realize that revolution is justified in the Declaration of Independence under special conditions—when a government becomes despotic and refuses to heed the peaceful petitions of its people for a redress of just grievances. "It is their right, it is their duty," states the Declaration, "to throw off such government and to provide new guards for their future security."

Those citizens who have advocated revolution in twentieth-century America, however, are only a small if highly vocal minority. They have not convinced the vast majority of Americans that their government is despotic, or that it is unwilling or unable to correct injustices in our society. But they serve the purpose of spotlighting those injustices and goading the Government to corrective action.

Most of us feel revulsion at genuine traitors who sell out their country to foreign powers, like Robert Best, Axis Sally, Lord Haw Haw (William Joyce) and Harry Gold. Often, however, they are emotionally warped individuals, frustrated in their lives and ambitions, and socially maladjusted. Perhaps it would be more humane to punish all such convicted traitors by imprisonment rather than by execution.

Sometimes, too, treason represents an unbearable choice between disloyalty and signing the death warrant for a man's family. Both Nazi Germany and the Soviet Union have forced American citizens to become spies on the threat of otherwise torturing or killing their relatives still in Europe.

Another argument in favor of flexible prison terms for treason is that the law can make mistakes, but a mistake cannot be corrected once a convicted defendant has been executed. If the Rosenbergs had been innocent, as they insisted and many investigators believed, a jail term instead of the death sentence would have given their defenders a greater opportunity to prove their innocence.

The value of the death penalty as a deterrent to treason has its defenders as well as its critics. It would be as difficult for either side to prove its case as to prove that the death penalty does or does not prevent murders.

Few lawyers would disagree, however, that it is harder to get a jury to convict a traitor if they know he may be put to death for what some may see as political reasons. Ironically, more real traitors would probably be prosecuted and convicted if the death penalty for treason were abolished.

Finally, how can all of us strengthen the bonds of loyalty we feel to each other as Americans, helping to reconcile the differences that polarize us and drive some dissenters to despair, others to acts of disloyalty?

It will certainly help if the Government regards dissenters as the "loyal opposition," listens respectfully to their arguments, and tries to accommodate their point of view at least to some extent. National unity is hardly helped when Government spokesmen attack dissenters as unpatriotic or traitorous or when police or National Guard troops use unwarranted force against protest demonstrations or kill students on campus.

At the same time responsible leaders of dissent need to police their own ranks to keep protest demonstrations nonviolent. A few hotheads throwing stones or breaking windows can provoke official violence and turn public sympathy away from the demonstrators. Change is far more likely to come about by means of dissenters who work peacefully within the political system than through the violence of revolutionaries.

All of us can help, too, by "cooling the rhetoric"—refraining from name-calling. To refer to the police as "pigs" or to dissenters as "a bunch of effete intellectual snobs" only intensifies the hostility on both sides.

We can also strengthen the bonds of loyalty in America by avoiding any insulting references to ethnic minority groups. Some German-Americans who had been insulted and derided during the hysteria of World War I became, in bitterness, fifth columnists for Nazi agents during the thirties and forties.

Some Italian Americans sneered at as "wops" or "dagoes" by fellow Americans became angry supporters of Mussolini. Some Nisei, treated contemptuously as "Japs" and thrown into American concentration camps, indignantly refused to swear loyalty to the United States during World War II. The race riots of the sixties and the rise of black militants sworn to violence against the white Establishment were in large part the fruit of two centuries of white oppression, insult, and scorn.

We must work harder at being Americans in the best sense, and that means becoming more tolerant of each other's different ethnic backgrounds and different views. We must not fall into the trap of confusing dissent with disloyalty or of defining only conformity as patriotism. The American flag belongs to all who live under it—those who support the Government as well as those who oppose the Government.

"We are a rebellious nation, our whole history is treason," abolitionist Theodore Parker reminded his fellow Americans. "Our blood was attainted before we were born; our creeds are infidelity to the mother church, our constitution treason to the fatherland."

Our Founding Fathers were never apologetic for their treason to England, considering it a glorious rebellion in the name of freedom. Had they lost the War of Independence, they would not be remembered today as great American patriots but only as unsuccessful British traitors. Well aware of this, they wrote the treason clause into the Constitution to make it extremely difficult to convict any American of treason.

"God forbid," wrote Thomas Jefferson, "we should ever be twenty years without such a rebellion. . . . What country can preserve its liberties if its rulers are not warned from time to time that this people preserve the spirit of resistance?"

It will always be arguable as to where dissent ends and disloyalty begins. We might suspect that any country that prosecutes too many citizens for conspiracy or treason tends to be totalitarian, whereas any country that prefers to engage dissenting citizens in public debate so that their arguments and proofs are compelled to survive or fall on their own merits is likely to be a free society.

Jeremy Bentham, the great English jurist who helped codify Britain's laws, declared that the way to tell a free government from a despotism is "the security with which malcontents may communicate their sentiments, concert their plans, and practice every mode of opposition short of actual revolt, before the executive power can be legally justified in disturbing them."

Perhaps that is the kind of perfect society all of us should strive for—a nation in which there is no need for violent protest, revolutionary activity, or disloyalty because every citizen has full opportunity for patriotic dissent, with the assurance that he is being heard and that the majority fully respects the rights of the minority.

Voltaire suggested the spirit of such a democracy when he wrote the beautiful oath of the free citizen: "I disapprove of what you say, but I will defend to the death your right to say it."

Bibliography

(* Indicates Recommended Reading)

*Archer, Jules, *Angry Abolitionist: William Lloyd Garrison.* New York: Julian Messner, 1969.

*———, *The Extremists: Gadflies of American Society.* New York: Hawthorn Books, Inc., 1969.

*———, *Hawks, Doves, and the Eagle.* New York: Hawthorn Books, Inc., 1970.

———, *Laws That Changed America.* New York: Criterion Books, 1967.

*———, *The Unpopular Ones.* New York: Crowell-Collier Press, 1968.

*———, *World Citizen: Woodrow Wilson.* New York: Julian Messner, 1967.

Baruch, Bernard M., *Baruch: The Public Years.* New York: Holt, Rinehart and Winston, 1960.

*Beirne, Francis F., *Shout Treason: The Trial of Aaron Burr.* New York: Hastings House Publishers, Inc., 1959.

*Bessie, Alvah, *Inquisition in Eden.* New York: The Macmillan Company, 1965.

187

Blackstock, Paul W., *Agents of Deceit*. Chicago: Quadrangle Books, 1966.

*Boveri, Margret, *Treason in the Twentieth Century*. New York: G. P. Putnam's Sons, 1963.

*Bulloch, John, *Akin to Treason*. London: Arthur Barker Limited, 1966.

*Carlson, John Roy, *Under Cover*. Cleveland and New York: World Publishing Company, 1943.

Carr, Albert Z., *The World and William Walker*. New York: Harper & Row, Publishers, 1963.

*Chambers, Whittaker, *Witness*. New York: Random House, 1952.

*Chapin, Bradley, *The American Law of Treason*. Seattle: University of Washington Press, 1964.

Chevalier, Haakon, *Oppenheimer: The Story of a Friendship*. New York: George Braziller, 1965.

De Toledano, Ralph, *Spies, Dupes, and Diplomats*. New Rochelle, New York: Arlington House, 1967.

————, and Lasky, Victor, *Seeds of Treason*. New York: Funk & Wagnalls Company, 1950.

Ducann, C. G. L., *Famous Treason Trials*. New York: Walker and Company, 1964.

Dulles, Allen, *The Craft of Intelligence*. New York: Harper & Row, Publishers, 1963.

*Forster, Arnold, and Epstein, Benjamin R., *Danger on the Right*. New York: Random House, 1964.

*Gentry, Curt, *Frame-Up: The Incredible Case of Tom Mooney and Warren Billings*. New York: W. W. Norton & Company, Inc., 1967.

*Grodzins, Morton, *The Loyal and the Disloyal*. Chicago: The University of Chicago Press, 1956.

*Hiss, Alger, *In the Court of Public Opinion*. New York: Alfred A. Knopf, 1957.

Holbrook, Stewart H., *The Dreamers of the American Dream*.

Garden City, New York: Doubleday & Company, Inc., 1957.

*Hoover, J. Edgar, *Masters of Deceit*. New York: Henry Holt and Company, 1958.

Klapp, Orrin E., *Symbolic Leaders*. Chicago: Aldine Publishing Company, 1964.

Krock, Arthur, *In the Nation: 1932–1966*. New York: Mc-Graw-Hill, Inc., 1966.

Lamparski, Richard, *Whatever Became Of . . . ?* New York: Crown Publishers, Inc., 1967.

*Lattimore, Owen, *Ordeal by Slander*. Boston: Little, Brown and Company, 1950.

Legislative Reference Service, Library of Congress, *Fascism in Action*. Washington: U.S. Government Printing Office, 1947.

Long, David F., *The Outward View*. Chicago: Rand McNally & Company, 1963.

*Markmann, Charles Lam, *The Noblest Cry: A History of the American Civil Liberties Union*. New York: St. Martin's Press, 1965.

Mazo, Earl, *Richard Nixon*. New York: Avon Books, 1960.

*Morray, Joseph P., *Pride of State*. Boston: Beacon Press, Inc., 1959.

*Myers, Gustavus, *History of Bigotry in the United States,* revised edition. New York: Capricorn Books, 1960.

*Newberry, Mike, *The Yahoos*. New York: Marzani and Munsell, 1964.

Reader's Digest, Secrets & Spies. Pleasantville, New York: The Reader's Digest Association, 1964.

*Root, Jonathan, *The Betrayers: The Rosenberg Case*. New York: Coward-McCann, Inc., 1963.

Rosner, Joseph, *The Hater's Handbook*. New York: Dell Publishing Co., Inc., 1967.

Rowan, Richard Wilmer, *The Story of Secret Service*. Garden

City, New York: Doubleday, Doran and Company, Inc., 1937.

*Seldes, George, *Facts and Fascism*. New York: In Fact, Inc., 1943.

*———, *One Thousand Americans*. New York: Boni & Gaer, 1947.

Seth, Ronald, *Secret Servants*. New York: Farrar, Straus and Cudahy, 1957.

Spolansky, Jacob, *The Communist Trail in America*. New York: The Macmillan Company, 1951.

*U.S. House of Representatives, Committee on Un-American Activities (HUAC), *Guerrilla Warfare Advocates in the United States*. Washington: U.S. Government Printing Office, 1968.

*———, *Subversive Influences in Riots, Looting, and Burning, Part 6 (San Francisco–Berkeley)*. Washington: U.S. Government Printing Office, 1969.

*———, *Subversive Involvement in Disruption of 1968 Democratic Party National Convention, Part 2*. Washington: U.S. Government Printing Office, 1968.

*West, Rebecca, *The New Meaning of Treason*. New York: The Viking Press, 1964.

*Wexley, John, *The Judgment of Julius and Ethel Rosenberg*. New York: Cameron & Kahn, 1955.

*Weyl, Nathaniel, *Treason*. Washington: Public Affairs Press, 1950.

*Wise, David, and Ross, Thomas B., *The Espionage Establishment*. New York: Random House, 1967.

Young, Kimball, *Isn't One Wife Enough?* New York: Henry Holt and Company, 1954.

Also consulted were issues of *The Nation, Newsweek,* and other periodicals, including publications of the American Civil Liberties Union, the far Right, and the New Left.

Index

191